Fathers, Sons, & Holy Ghosts:

Baseball as a Spiritual Experience

Austin Gisriel

ISBN: 1542677343
ISBN-13: 978-1542677349

DEDICATION

To the nine-year old in each of us.

CONTENTS

ACKNOWLEDGMENTS

I am happy to acknowledge my random collection of sources and inspiration!

Al Smith and I started playing baseball together our sophomore year at Loch Raven High School in the spring of 1973 and we're still at it. We've attended baseball games, and located the best barbecue shacks from Virginia to Florida to Nebraska and back. None of this would have been as much fun without you, Al.

Mo Weber, you taught me more about the game in the time I've known you than I had learned in my previous 51 years. No one will break your record of consecutive seasons leading the league in stolen gloves. And yes, it is wonderful to be in Indiana.

Thanks to fellow author David B. Stinson whose reverence for baseball's temples is second to none. It's always a pleasure to talk to you and share a baseball experience or three. Thanks for allowing me to share a couple of yours.

Thanks to Walt Friedman of Summer Game Books who offered valuable comments on the manuscript.

Thanks to Lynne Marino and Lizzy Kipps and her family for sharing their family baseball stories in one form or another.

Thanks to Mary Uebelhor who welcomed Al and me to League Stadium in Huntingburg, Indiana on the hottest night of the 2015 Ohio Valley League season. Folks such as you and the Kipps family are the true care tenders of collegiate summer ball.

Martha, you have shared this ride from the Orioles 25th Anniversary game, which led to my first published writing, past the 60th Anniversary, to this. Now, for another World Series title. Maybe granddaughter Riley will bring the Birds some luck?

Becky, I am still proud of you for making the Conococheague Minor League All-Star team. And to think your first year you managed only a walk and a foul ball. We've shared many wonderful baseball memories and I look forward to taking Riley to her first game. I'm also proud of you for teaching Jesse to love the game. I couldn't ask more from a son-

i

in-law than to love my daughter and talk baseball with her dad!

Sarah, when you were little you once remarked that "baseball is my other sibling." That's worthy of acknowledgement right there.

Lisa Schwarz, you know what you did for me! Thank you.

To Mr. Wade, my former Sunday School teacher, and next door neighbor; and to all the adults who were an important part of my baseball tableau when I was a kid, thank you.

To all the kids I played with and no doubt annoyed because I *knew* I was the best kid on the team (for a while). I apologize and thank you for all those games, and games of three-flies in, and run down, and up-against-the-wall.

Dad, you never missed a game and you made sure I had gloves and bats and someone who was always there to cheer me on. And that new, white ball from Montgomery Wards in the spring. Thanks.

Mom, you rooted for the Orioles right to the end when you left the present and returned to those days of your youth in old Oriole Park; you washed all those uniforms and rearranged suppers and vacations so I could play ball. Thanks.

.

A BRIEF INTRODUCTION

No other sport, and indeed few other activities evoke as much passion as does baseball. It is a passion that unites generations and genders, laborers and lawyers, Republicans and Democrats. Baseball serves as a common language, a unified way of perceiving the world, a means to greater understanding. For many baseball people, the game is really a spiritual experience, a phrase that I use very deliberately. Baseball's shrines, rituals, myths, and heroes certainly give it a religious aura. Many activities, however, may be pursued "religiously." A true spiritual experience goes beyond shrines, rituals, myths, and heroes; it shows us the Eternal in every moment. It opens our eyes to the possibility of something Grand in even the most ordinary moments, which of course are the kind of moments that comprise most of our lives.

Many authors have detailed the spiritual experience that is baseball and some filmmakers have even used the game as a metaphor for spiritual concepts such as redemption, a concept at the heart of *Field of Dreams*. Certainly other sports have their own shrines, rituals, myths, and heroes, but no one, however, has yet made a movie about Johnny Unitas emerging from a cornfield to throw a touchdown pass to his father. The real question is w*hy* does baseball engender such a strong spiritual response?

One could apply psychology, anthropology, and religion to answer

1

this question. I have a degree in psychology and another one in theology, but mostly I have majored in baseball as I have matriculated through Life. The best way to answer the question as to why baseball has such a spiritual effect on people is to mix personal observations on the game with a dash of psychology and a couple tablespoons of theology to validate the flavor. While the ingredients are unique to my recipe, the taste should be familiar to any baseball person.

I use the term *baseball person* rather than fan, because *fan* is just too limited. Writers, announcers, coaches, and the players themselves respond spiritually to the game as well, an experience typified by the "good-bye" tweet of pitcher Dan Haren when he announced his retirement on October 21, 2015:

Thank you baseball. I played this beautiful game for 30 years. I took my jersey off for the last time tonight. It was an honor.

Indeed, it is often the experience of the players, their heroics and their failures that give depth to the game's spirituality. More on that later.

Upon finishing this little book, you may think, *Well, that was a random selection of sources*, and you would be correct. We are all a random selection of sources and this work is very much a personal reflection. I could have used my degrees more formally and presented a psycho-religious treatise on the spiritual nature of baseball, but the mere thought of writing that bores me; reading it would be unbearable. The hold that baseball has on people is best explained anecdotally, not academically.

I grew up outside of Baltimore and so many of my personal experiences and references involve the Orioles. I've been an Oriole fan and a baseball fan all my life and as many fans do, I have folders full of articles about why the game is so special. I have referenced some of those clippings.

I taught high school English and got pretty good at mining themes from stories and I've referenced some of that.

I know some people and contacted others, and I referenced some of them. Often, a good source for any project actually turns out to be "this guy I know."

It's kind of like Howard Sensel wrote in *Baseball and the Cold War*, a book published in 1977 and one that I'd never heard of until my friend, Al Smith, whom you'll meet later, saw it at a flea market in Florida, bought it, read it, and passed it along to me. (You see what I mean about our lives being a random collection of sources?) Anyway, Sensel wrote:

The evidence is that there are depths beyond which an intellectual process cannot go. The evidence is that there are aspects of your own identity so strongly established that they cannot be penetrated by conviction, not to mention thought. There are things about our own identity that we cannot alter by decision. And baseball is one of those things.[1]

In other words, baseball is mysticism, not theology, which is why the best explanation for our spiritual reaction to baseball is a personal one. While it is difficult to explain the mystical, I need only reference the thrill that is produced when seeing that green, green grass upon exiting the concourse and entering the grand stand. All baseball people know what I'm talking about. I keep asking myself, why is that? What is it in us that reacts to that lush lawn with the dirt diamond in one corner? Keep in mind I've only got one ticket to a single seat, but here is my ballpark explanation from where I'm sitting.

1 IN THE BEGINNING

Whether you flunk out of Little League or end up in the Hall of Fame, most of us share the same first baseball experience, which is a simple game of catch.

Baseball author David Laurila wrote an entry for the August 31, 2011 blog *FanGraphs* entitled "Playing Catch and the 'Rhythm of the Universe,'" in which he interviewed a dozen or so major leaguers on why playing catch is so much fun.[2] Almost every player mentioned that playing catch, even now that they do it "professionally," so to speak, takes them back to childhood, to their buddies, to their dads. Pitcher Andrew Bailey[3] was quoted as saying,

The love you have for the game really starts with playing catch. Being out there in the back yard playing catch with your father or friends is kind of the first step to falling in love with the game of baseball. It takes you back to those days every single time you get on a big-league field and do it.

Growing up, it's 'Let's go out and play catch,' and now the game has obviously evolved to more than that. There are days when you stop and think about it — how far you've come from riding your bike to the park and playing catch with your buddies.[4]

Playing catch is baseball's most basic ritual and hearkens to humanity's primitive days when the body *was* the temple of the Lord. Humanity's "physical acts, are unquestionably older than his words and more primal expressions of his feeling that the god is present," according to German scholar Walter Otto.[5] It is ironic to note, now that we have constructed actual temples, that we compel ourselves to sit still within them. Everyone from the whirling dervishes to the practitioners of tantric yoga, however, understand that the body is a vessel by which we may reach that Something that is greater than oneself. Indeed famed mythologist Joseph Campbell argues that what we seek in life is not meaning, but the "experience of being alive, so that our life experiences on the purely physical plane will have resonances within our own innermost being and reality, so that we actually feel the rapture of being alive."[6]

Like the game itself, playing catch seems to render Time irrelevant, and it may be that such irrelevance is necessary to the "rapture of being alive." American theologian, Paul Tillich expressed such a concept in his landmark essay, "The Lost Dimension in Religion." That "lost dimension" according to Tillich is *depth*. Lamenting modern preoccupation with "the mere movement ahead without an end," he cautions that "no one can experience depth without stopping and becoming aware of himself."

Earl Weaver might have called this "deep depth."

Diane Ackerman, an award-winning poet, essayist, and naturalist calls this "deep play." In her 1999 book entitled *Deep Play*, she writes, "Deep play always involves the sacred and holy. . . . We spend our lives in pursuit of moments that will allow these altered states to happen."[7] A two-out, two-strike, game-winning home run, a birthday ballgame with Dad, all that green grass. Such moments seem to fall to us as children and we spend the rest of our lives hoping to collect a few more. The quest even becomes an inheritance: Consider the case of Wayne Williams whose father became a Cubs fan while stationed at the Great Lakes Naval Training Station during World War II. Wayne, Sr. died in 1980, but the two had made a pact that if the Cubs ever went to the World Series, they would watch it together. With the Cubs needing one win to clinch the 2016 World Series, Wayne drove 600 miles to his father's grave in order to share Game Seven. Williams sat quietly, streaming the game on his phone, the beam from a flashlight illuminating his dad's marker.[8] While his dad may not have been present, there is no doubt that this was indeed a father and son moment spent in an "altered state."

Deep play is "akin to rapture and ecstasy, that humans relish, even require, to feel whole,"[9] says Ackerman who later notes that, "One problem with religion today is that it is mainly non-religious. We have lost the distinction between true religious experience and belonging to an organized religion."[10]

Tillich writes,

As long as the preliminary, transitory concerns are not silenced, no matter how interesting and valuable and important they may be, the voice of the ultimate concern cannot be heard. This is the deepest root of the loss of the dimension of depth in our period—the loss of religion in its basic and universal meaning.[11]

To that end, catch may be the perfect ritualization of depth. Once you let the ball go, there is nothing you can do but watch it sail toward your partner. Once he lets it go, there is nothing you can do, but await its arrival. Time is no longer linear, but circular, a concept perfectly illustrated by the denouement of *Field of Dreams* in which Ray Kinsella and his long-since deceased father play catch. Ray's dad appears as a young man, yet perfectly aware that he *is* Ray's dad. Ray now truly experiences his father as both father and as a young man before fatherhood and responsibility and time have worn him down. Linear time is completely removed from the equation, which gives depth to their game of catch. Naturally, this removal does not bother the characters, but interestingly, it does not seem to bother the audience, either, because the audience instinctively responds to this vicarious restoration of depth.

Before the climactic game of catch, James Earl Jones as Terrance Mann delivers the soliloquy that renders misty, baseball fans everywhere, the "People will come," speech. Explaining why people will visit Ray's diamond in the middle of the cornfield, author W. P. Kinsella through Jones as Mann delivers a line that would inspire Paul Tillich to do the wave: "For it is money they have, and peace they lack."[12]

In the Major League Baseball special, *Field of Dreams: Twenty-five Years Later*, hosted by Bob Costas, actor Kevin Costner, who played Ray

Kinsella, explained the power of that soliloquy: "The words were baseball poetry and actually framed the game. Gave it a level of logic to guys who can't explain why they like the game and their wives are going, 'Why do you watch? It's too long [etc.]' and all of a sudden it's like 'Listen to the speech. Listen to the speech.'"[13]

Baseball people understand that the game is one of subtlety, of thoughtfulness, of depth. Each game will proceed at its own pace and that the "progress" of each game may develop slowly or quickly; it may hinge on a single pitch or on an entire series of plays stretched out over several innings. Baseball people will note on their scorecards whether a run crossed home plate, but they will note in their hearts the fact that on that same play, with the second baseman and shortstop in a double cutoff for a throw to third, the right fielder raced in to cover second, just in case the batter/runner, who had taken second on the throw that in fact went to home, rounded the bag too far.

Mr. Alan Koontz, from Berkley Springs, West Virginia, and whose letter to the editor some 24 years ago made it into one of my files, put it well when he wrote

The most intense action in a typical game is not visible to the naked eye. It requires a knowledge of the game's ins and outs that gives the fans the ability to make out the heated engagements taking place in what by all appearances is nothing more than a tableau vivant. *Indeed, anyone just looking for action is bound to miss the best part altogether.*[14]

It is interesting to note that the field in Dyersville, Iowa where *Field of Dreams* was shot, has been preserved, and to visit has become something of a pilgrimage for many, the object for whom, once they get there is to play catch on the field. The 25th Anniversary celebration of *Field of Dreams* was held, appropriately enough, over Father's Day Weekend in 2014 and included concerts, celebrity softball games, and even a showing of the movie on an outdoor screen on the diamond itself; but the chance to play catch on this now sanctified patch of grass was the focal point for most. This fact was not lost on Costner who, acting as something of a priest, aided participants in the ritual. After playing catch with his own children he told Costas:

I couldn't help but notice, not children, but there were grown men

at the end; and they all had their gloves and they were just watching. I said to my son, "I'm going to play catch with these men." And he looked up and said, "All of 'em?" And I said, "Well, let's see what happens." And he went over and sat down and I pointed at one guy and I threw to him and after 8 or 9 catches he stopped himself and he gave another man a turn. And one by one I probably played with 30 guys.[15]

As the MLB camera panned the field showing would-be ballplayers of all ages, sizes, and abilities tossing a baseball back and forth, co-star Timothy Busfield, who played Mark, Kinsella's disbelieving brother-in-law said, "There's a magic to this field that wasn't there when we were shooting. This was just a film location. You can feel it out there. You can feel the film out there."[16]

Naturally, the MLB special concluded the same way that the film did: Costner and actor Dwier Brown, who played John Kinsella, Ray's father, had another game of catch, twenty-five years after their first game of catch.

The entire movie is based on, as Costner explained, this game of catch, and it has resonated so powerfully that the score, written by James Horner, is used whenever teams celebrate their former heroes who are either retiring or brought back for an old-timers game. No explanation for the music is necessary and merely the opening strains have been known to bring men to tears.

"It is like a dog whistle for men's emotions," Busfield told Costas. "They can't hold back. I saw a tear in your [Bob Costas'] eye last night [while viewing the film on the field]. I was moved, I was crying and I know what's going on!"[17] Such overwhelming emotion is an indication that the "rapture of being alive" is taking place and that our innermost being, no longer weary of the world or caring to be cool, is free to run around in his short pants and express what he truly feels.

The "little film" as Costner described it, about a game of catch, resonates so well that the Portland Sea Dogs of the Class AA Eastern League, hold an annual season-ending "Field of Dreams" game in which their players, mimicking the players in the movie by wearing early 20th century uniforms, emerge from corn stalks placed along the center field fence before the game as a way of thanking the fans for supporting them during the year.

Movie ghosts, or in this particular case, the Portland Sea Dogs, emerging from the corn ritualize a phenomenon that all baseball fans have experienced: the ghosts that emerge from our memories. Some, stand before us in their youthful glory and in our collective memories. And so, for example, if you throw out the name of Tito Landrum to a congregation of Oriole fans who are in their forties or older, everyone will smile and some will reflexively repeat the name, for to speak of the devil or to call upon the Lord, is to make him appear. And so he does, standing there in the right hand batter's box on a gray and chilly Chicago afternoon in the fall of 1983 in the 10th inning of a scoreless and crucial Game 4 of the American League Championship Series. Obtained from the Cardinals on August 31st, Landrum drove an 0-1 pitch from Britt Burns deep into the left field stands. That home run would propel Baltimore to a 3-0 victory and the American League pennant.

Landrum's time in the spotlight, however, was short-lived. He never garnered a single plate appearance for the Orioles during their five-game World Series win over Philadelphia and was traded back to St. Louis the following March. Released by the Dodgers in 1987 and again in 1988 by the Cardinals, with whom he was by this time serving his third hitch, he was once more picked up by the Orioles in April of 1988 only to be released in May, his big league career finished. . . . But that day, that October 8th, that top of the 10th . . . the suddenness with which the ball left old Comiskey and with which the game was no longer scoreless, well that moment is *alive* and that is the definition of *eternal*. It's not that a moment is immortal, that it is incapable of dying; it's that a moment is *still* living. That's eternal.

Other ghosts emerge from private memories and stand before us in the glory of our own youth. When Ray Kinsella recognizes that the catcher in the final scene of *Field of Dreams* is his dad, his wife and the other ballplayers recede from the scene and from the present so that Ray and John could share this game of catch that was not quite in the present, and not quite in the past, but was "beyond time," as Campbell might put it.[18]

Baseball is one of our few doorways to the Eternal because the game is a moment to moment process. This is just like Life, but as Tillich has pointed out, we're too preoccupied with "the mere movement ahead without an end." The pace and deliberation of the game, however, make us mindful, not only of ourselves, but of the possibility of the moment.

There exists a classic photo of Roger Maris' 61st home run that perfectly illustrates this idea. Only, it's not a photo of the homer itself. When I first saw it at the Hall of Fame in Cooperstown, the photo was in the form of life-sized cut outs of Maris, home plate umpire Bill Kinnamon, and Red Sox catcher Russ Nixon. Nixon is rising out of his crouch and Maris has just followed through on his swing and is beginning to leave the batter's box. All three are looking in the same direction and if you drew a line from the respective eyes of each, they would intersect at the ball, out there somewhere beyond the photograph and still in flight. In our collective memories that ball has yet to land, because it is the perfect moment when possibility is about to become reality. It's a sure thing, but it has not yet arrived and so it may be savored. It is the tasting of the moment and not its consumption that leaves that indelible mark on the memory. It is just such moments in which Diane Ackerman's concept of deep play occurs, moments in which, "The past never happened and the future won't arise. One is suspended between tick and tock."[19]

The Maris photo is black and white, which is perfect. Other sports have become high-definition, surround sound videos full of mere movement ahead, but baseball remains a black and white photo. We each have our own personal angle on the game depending on where we sit and who we root for. We each have that special person in our lives who taught us how to play catch. Those black and white moments become Eternal because it is we, and not the sponsors or the networks, who color them with our own personal pallets and set them in motion again and again with our own imaginations.

Howard Sensel in his eccentric, but insightful memoir, *Baseball and the Cold War*, wrote, "We have lost our sense of tradition, and with that we are in danger of forgetting the past. If we do this, we are depriving ourselves of the only possibility for depth in human experience.

Memory and depth are the same thing."[20]

Baseball never lacks for memory or tradition, which was part of Sensel's basic thesis. The value of baseball's traditions lies in the fact that they establish order in a chaotic world as all religious traditions attempt to do. Anthropologist Anthony F. C. Wallace stated that ritual reduces the overwhelming amount of complexity of life into that which can be comprehended.[21] Or as Bill Veeck once said, "Baseball is almost the only orderly thing in a very unorderly world. If you get three strikes, even the best lawyer in the world can't get you off."

Fans stretch after the top of the 7th inning. Pitchers stand 60'6" from home plate rather than an even 60' because of a surveyor's error, one that could easily be corrected but hey, it's tradition now. There are eight warm up pitches given to each pitcher by Official Rule 8.03, although in the rule book they are referred to as "preparatory pitches." The rule book itself is a Deuteronomic code of traditions and no facet of the game is too small to be included. For example, Rule 3.01f states that "Before the game begins the umpire shall ensure that an official rosin bag shall be placed on the ground behind the pitcher's plate prior to the start of each game." I bet somewhere in some league sometime over the past 150 years, there's been an argument about whether the rosin bag was really an "official" one. The art of arguing with an umpire is a tradition just as never winning an argument with an umpire is a tradition and a sociologist might reasonably conclude that many baseball people oppose instant replay because it removes one of baseball's more colorful traditions from the game. Precision is not the same thing as order. Watching Earl Weaver tear up the rule book as he did on the field in Cleveland one night is a highlight-reel example of a wonderful tradition; watching one umpire watch the second umpire don a headset to find out if the third umpire got a call right is not only untraditional, it offers no sense of the moment; no opportunity to experience depth. The call will be precise, but the process is not orderly.

In spiritual terms, baseball represents an almost mystical— certainly a mystifying—combination of the sacred and the profane, although the latter term is better translated as "the ordinary." Life does the same thing, but because we lack depth, that is because we pursue only the next result, we have forgotten how to recognize the sacred. We journey along waiting to encounter a burning bush, but completely miss the sparks that have lit the way. Baseball has plenty of burning bushes, usually encapsulated by numbers; any baseball fan can tell you the significance of 511, 56, .406 or 61, although some disciples will insist that 61 was extinguished and replaced with 73.[22] (Those in favor of 61 will insist that the burning bush of 73 was falsely inflamed with steroids.) Baseball is full of sparks; every game is flush with sparks. A few of them may turn into burning bushes, but it is the sparks that baseball people savor. It's why we remember Tito Landrum as well as Roger Maris. It's why the softest of loopers may result in a hit that wins the World Series a la Luis Gonzalez in 2001 or a screaming line drive that may result in its final out a la Willie McCovey in 1962. You never know, but you *always* believe.

I've been to World Series and playoff games and Oriole Opening Days, but indeed, the game that stands out as the most fun and most interesting that I ever attended was a game of no particular consequence in Greensboro, North Carolina in 2006. My family and I had traveled there from our home in Maryland (at the time) for a wedding. When we checked into our hotel, we discovered that Greensboro's then new ballpark was only three blocks away. With time to kill, we walked down to take a look and configured as it is, with the outfield wall right along North Eugene Street, batting practice home run balls were flying over that wall and into the street. We picked up several. One woman stopped her car at the stop sign, leaned out the door and picked up one or two. Becky, our older daughter, a veteran of the Conococheague Little League, and a former Hagerstown Suns Promotions Girl looked at me. I looked at her, thinking the same thing. We had to get out of going to the rehearsal dinner and get to the game that night.

Becky has always been a baseball fan ever since she was in utero. The first time that my wife Martha felt Becky kick was on June 28, 1987. Becky was reacting to me yelling at Tom Niedenfuer blow a 7-4 lead in the bottom of the ninth by yielding back-to-back-to-back home runs to the Tigers in Detroit.[23] (As for our younger daughter, Sarah, I don't know what happened. She has only a passing interest in baseball, but is, at least, a huge Adam Jones fan. She also has sworn that she will name one of her sons "Brooks" after Brooks Robinson her father's hero, a gesture that means far more to me than if she names him *Austin*.)

Grandsons are in the future, however.[24] Back in Greensboro, when we returned to the hotel I looked at Martha, who didn't even wait for me to present our case. She simply told us to go have a good time. Did we ever. One of the few things better than going to the ballpark with your son is taking your daughter, especially one who can keep score, find the best concession stand, and drink in the majesty of all that green grass. And we weren't at a rehearsal dinner, although ironically, there were two wedding parties at the game along with thousands of others because it was a Friday Fireworks Night, which just added to our delight.

The Greensboro Grasshoppers were taking on the Greenville Drive in South Atlantic League action on this July 7th and as Fortune was apparently favoring us, we saw the strangest play that either of us has ever witnessed and that includes some of the odd things that took place in the Conococheague Little League.

In the bottom of the 4th, Greensboro loaded the bases with none out when catcher Brett Hayes crushed a long fly ball to deep left center. Everyone in the ballpark thought it was a grand slam when Greenville center fielder Jay Johnson made a spectacular leaping catch running into the wall in the process. Stunned, he crumpled to the ground, but had presence of mind to flip the ball to left fielder Chris Turner. Meanwhile, the base runners, assuming as we did that the ball was at least good for extra bases were scurrying hither and yon. Turner threw the ball to second where Andy Jenkins was doubled off the bag for a highly unusual 8-7-4 putout. Second baseman Matt Mercurio, presuming that the man on third had never tagged up, threw to third, the umpire raised his arm, and we all thought that we had witnessed a triple play.

The runner on first, Kris Harvey was already half way to third and he was desperately making his way back to first--retouching second on the way--as the ball was being thrown to third. Harvey made it safely and planted himself on the bag as the Drive walked off the field, but suddenly, the umpires began to talk to each other. They had seen something that we had not. The runner on third Jeff Van Houten, had indeed tagged and scored and therefore, Greenville executed a double play, but not a triple play. Had Mercurio thrown to first, which he could have easily done, *then* it would have been a triple play.

The final result was that Hayes had hit into a double play sacrifice fly that began with what Greensboro manager, Brandon Hyde, described in the paper the next day as "the best catch of the year. Might be the best I've seen in four years." Center fielder Johnson provided a wonderfully typical baseball quote when he said, "It happened so quick that I couldn't tell you what happened."[25]

This play tied the score at 1-1 and ironically enough, Greensboro took the lead in the 7th on a routine sacrifice fly to center and won the game 2-1.

The fireworks burst over our heads as we walked back to our hotel, but they could not match the sparks of magic that we had seen during the game. An inherent attribute of baseball is its ability to amaze, to spark—so to speak—wonder, and wonder is an inherent attribute of children and children accept magic as a matter of course.

And so, baseball, unconsciously draws us in a spiritual direction. It teaches us to be ready for the divine to enter our ordinary world and trust me; a sacrifice fly into a double-play that was almost a triple play two different ways is divine. That's not to say that every game will contain such a play or be a thriller or be historic. The *potential* for thrills or history may begin on any pitch, however. If our expectation of the divine, which is another way of saying the fulfillment of our faith, does not take place in some routine, 6-2 ballgame, then we have at the very least, exercised our faith so that it is strong when the big moment arrives. Faith may not always be rewarded, but as New York Met reliever Tug McGraw once famously said, "You gotta believe!" It's not the result of our believing—Mighty Casey all too often does strike out—it's the exercise of believing that gives our lives depth.

Indeed, Emile Durkheim, a pioneer in the field of sociology wrote in *The Elementary Forms of Religious Life*, that religion is not idealistic, but rather realistic and that within the Christian tradition, even Satan, while he may be impure, is not "profane," again in the sense of not ordinary.[26] So it is in baseball that winning is not the only sacred aspect of the game. Losing is, too. With the exception of a few historic outliers, every team will lose 61 games every year. Hall of Famer Reggie Jackson struck out 2,597 times in his career. Given that he averaged 656 plate appearances per season, you could say that he spent four years of his career never putting the ball in play. The greatest hitter in the game, Ty Cobb, failed at a rate of 63.3%.

Durkheim went on to say that,

All is to be found there, and if in the majority of cases we see the good victorious over evil, life over death, the powers of light over the powers of darkness, it is because reality is not otherwise. If the relation between these two contrary forces were reversed, life would be impossible, but, as a matter of fact, it maintains itself and even tends to develop.[27]

When Durkheim used the word *there* in the above quote, he was referring to religion, but it applies to baseball. "Wait 'til next year!" is a creed, and the function of creed is "to point to the ultimate"[28] which transcends any statement or ritual. Winning next year may strengthen our faith, but should we lose next season, too, our faith is not diminished. Famed baseball writer Thomas Boswell once wrote, "The sanguine baseball fan knows, of course, that his game, more than most, is not about the final score. It's about the stories along the way. Yes, just like life, where you know the final score before you start. Death wins. So what? Let's play."[29]

Ironically enough, Boswell wrote this in March of 1989, in an article entitled, "The Bums of Summer," in which he assumed, logically enough, that the Baltimore Orioles, coming off a 107 loss season in 1988 would be terrible, with the chance to be historically futile. By July, and with the Orioles in first place, Boswell wrote a piece entitled, "There's Joy in Birdland," the third paragraph of which reads succinctly, "Oh, me of little faith."

Baseball connoisseur that he is Boswell went on to write,

"Does it really matter whether the Orioles continue to amaze us? Isn't it enough that they have already made us wonder about the limits

of renewed wonder? If the O's can do what they have already done, then how much might we accomplish ourselves with a similar change of attitude, a comparable rebirth of enthusiasm and willed innocence?"[30]

In contrast, a home and food writer for *The Sun* in Baltimore, Karol V. Menzie once wrote, "Some things can't be begun again. Childhood, innocence, love once it's gone wrong." Of course, *she* was wrong, a fact she admitted in a brief and beautiful essay entitled, "Hey Daddy I Made The Bigs."

Menzie had won a company-picnic prize of throwing out the ceremonial first pitch at an Oriole game. Her father, an ardent baseball fan, had taught her many important lessons including how to pitch. He was deceased almost 30 years when his daughter took the mound at Memorial Stadium:

I wanted to tell him how it felt. How green the grass is, and how clean it smells. How loudly the balls smack into gloves. How quiet it is on the field, no matter how many fans are roaring their heads off upstairs. How big the mascot looks and how serious the players seem. The cool feel of the ball in my bare hand, the sense that for all the spectators above, the man with the glove and I are there alone.

I had, instead, to offer him a little prayer: Dear Daddy, I haven't thrown a baseball in 35 years. I'm afraid I'll hit the mascot or drop the ball or bean the cameraman or forget to let go or fall over my own feet. So do you think you could just lean down from the Big Yard where you play now and give me a nudge? A hint? I want you to be proud of me. I'm listening real hard 'cause I know you're here. I know you wouldn't miss it for the world.[31]

Life is not the movies, not quite, anyway. If Karol's dad did not appear on the field to play catch with her the way that John Kinsella did with Ray, is there any doubt that for her, he was there? In the time it took for the ball to reach home plate, time ceased altogether. Eternal is beyond time and Eternity is where our innermost beings live and we can get there with a simple game of catch.

2 YOU GOTTA BELIEVE

When I was two years old, according to the story that my parents always told me, I could stand up in my playpen and throw a ball across the room. I have no reason to doubt the veracity of that story, but I'm not about to research whether such a feat is possible for a two year old. I have always taken that tale as part of my personal mythology, like Hercules strangling the snakes in his crib when he was two. It was clear: My Destiny was baseball.

My parents would take me on visits to my grandfather who was institutionalized in what we then called a nursing home, the victim of a stroke. He had been offered a contract to play for the Eastern League Baltimore Orioles when he was young, but his mother refused to let him sign because the Orioles played baseball on Sundays. My grandfather became a minister, but according to my dad, *his* dad always yearned to play ball. I have a vague sense, given what I know about Oriole history and my grandfather's birthdate that this story doesn't add up, but I will never do the math. Myths don't have to contain facts, they have to contain truth.

Regardless, the thing my grandfather responded to most after his stroke was me throwing a ball across the room, and *that* must be true because I remember how my father's face would light up at the memory of how *his* son had connected with *his* father.

Is that the wellspring of my passion for the game of baseball? Did the delight I gave a sick old man somehow get inside me and make me want to deliver this delight to everyone by playing ball?

I certainly wanted to please my dad who took such pride in his only child, and playing baseball was an easy, natural way for me to do that. At least it was until the other boys started outgrowing me around age 14. Until then, I *was* the best kid on the team.

My father rarely missed any games even when I was playing for Loch Raven High School and he was the principal of Overlea High School, both in Baltimore County, Maryland. Loch Raven's diamond was, and still is, set in a hollow, and behind home plate was "Dad's Hill." There was my dad, Al Smith's dad, and Bob Stagge's dad. Almost always it was just the three of them, never hollering, just watching quietly. We'd come to bat and feel the pride emanating from that hill.

***

Yes, Al and I have been friends since we started playing ball together in 10th grade. We got married within 13 days of each other, we raised our families, we buried our fathers within six months of each other. All through the years, all through the *decades* baseball has been the common denominator. Growing up outside of Baltimore, we've been life-long Oriole fans. Even now, that Al lives 1,000 miles away in Florida, if he's watching the Orioles and something good or something bad happens, the phone will ring. We skip the "hellos" as that would be superfluous and immediately begin discussing the play that we have both witnessed.

I have never said the words, "I love you" to Al nor has he to me, but that has never been necessary. That's what the phone says when it rings like that.

***

Maybe my passion for the game came from my mother, who as a high school girl would go with her friend Edith to Old Oriole Park, as it is still known by the few who remember it, to see the International League Orioles play. As about the only girls in the place, Mrs. Jack Dunn, the owner's wife, would invite them to sit with her in her box. (The ticket stubs and autographs in my possession make this story highly probable.) Maybe my passion for the game was passed along in some genetic form; a "base" gene from my mother and a "ball" gene from my grandfather. Al and I often introduce ourselves as "non-genetic" twins, but maybe we both received that same set of genes. His mom still follows the Orioles rather religiously and his dad, Albert E. Smith III (I'm Austin E. Gisriel, Jr.) was a catcher on the Southern High School team that featured an outfielder by the name of Al Kaline.

Perhaps my passion for the game was derived from my environment which was very adult-oriented from the beginning. My mother was 40 when she had me in 1957, a highly unusual age to be having children in those days, and is it turns out, I was the only child. I was around adults as often as I was around kids, and baseball was a way to connect with them. It was a common language even if I was not a very sophisticated speaker at the time. I certainly couldn't carry on a conversation about Nikita Krushchev or the civil rights movement, but I could about baseball. In the summer of 1964, when I was seven, the Orioles, by now somehow, *my* Orioles were in first place, but by the time school started in the fall, the Yankees were surging. Each morning, I would open the sports pages of *The Morning Sun* and see that **ORIOLES** was printed in bold, capital letters at the top of the American League standings. One morning in September, before I walked to school, they were not. I can see that breakfast table and feel the despair even now.

In October, with the Yankees playing the Cardinals in the World Series, my mother took me to a department store in downtown Baltimore and left me in the television department to watch the game on one of the true miracles of the age, a color television. I remember quietly urging on the Cardinals because the enemy of my enemy, i.e. the Yankees, is my friend. An older gentleman (who was no doubt younger than I am now) seemed quite pleased with me. "That's a good boy," he said, "Never root for the Yankees," or words to that effect. Whatever the exact words were, I still live by their spirit. This was the first time I understood that I might have something in common with a total stranger.

I went to my first game that next summer. I remember sitting on the floor playing my Cadaco All-Star Baseball Game when my dad came home and announced that we had tickets to see the Orioles play the Red Sox at Memorial Stadium that night. The Red Sox had a pitcher named Bill Monbouquette who also appeared on a Cadaco All-Star Baseball Game disc (the game was played with spinners; a player's disc slipped over the spinner and after spinning it "just right," the result was known). Dad said that he was starting that night. I remember, also that I wanted to see Dick Radatz, a huge man (for the time) and a real fireballer (for the time) and that he did get in the game and the Orioles did win. I looked up the game on baseball-reference.com and sure enough, on June 24, Bill Monboquette gave up four runs in four innings in a 4-1 Oriole win. Radatz pitched the eighth and Brooks Robinson hit a two-run homer in the first and finished the contest with three runs batted in.

My earliest ticket stub, however, is from a month later, a July 23, 1965 game against the Minnesota Twins. Steve Barber had shut out Minnesota for seven innings when Bob Allison and Earl Battey hit back-to-back homers to lead off the 8th. Tied at 2-2 heading into the bottom of the 9th, Charlie Lau, pinch-hitting for Barber, drew a leadoff walk from Jim Perry. A Bob Johnson single and a walk to Norm Siebern loaded the bases with one out, bringing Brooks Robinson to the plate. He singled to center on a 1-2 count to score pinch runner Luis Aparicio for a dramatic victory.

I didn't remember any of that; had to look up the game on baseball-reference.com, but when I did, I was immediately struck by the thought that it must have been this game that led me to believe in Baseball Magic. My hero, Brooks Robinson, really did deliver a game-winning, 9th inning base hit just as he always did when my baseball cards were spread out on the floor and an imaginary game was taking place, my finger tracking the arc of the invisible ball.[32] Maybe it was that one game that permanently fixed my passion for baseball. I might also mention that Steve Barber, the Orioles first 20-game winner, and I were born in the same hospital, Takoma Park Adventist. That was another divine sign of my impending major league stardom as far as I was concerned.

I distinctly remember a different kind of magic that took place probably at that Friday night game against the Twins. The concourse at Memorial Stadium was open and my dad lifted me up to look out and view the lights of the city. What a thrill! Lights as far as I could see! That's when I first learned that by raising yourself up a little, you could really see more than you ever imagined was there.

Magic on the field. Magic lights. And then a magical year. The Orioles won it all in 1966 and I sat in Section 39, Row 13, Seat 10 in the upper deck to watch Wally Bunker shut out the Dodgers in Game Three. Another distinct memory: When Paul Blair stepped to the plate in the 6th inning, I yelled, "C'mon Paul! You can do it!" And he did. A long home run to left center field. The old men—again probably much younger than I am now—who sat nearby were thrilled by my cheering, make that my incantation. One of them, with a big grin, said to me, "You said he could do it!" That's when I first learned that you could influence the magic, if you cheered the right cheer or sat just so in front of the television. By 1989, I discovered that my remote control could influence the magic. After being not only the worst team in baseball, but enduring a 21-game losing streak to open the 1988 season, the Orioles would go to Toronto for the final weekend of play in 1989 with a shot at the division crown. I couldn't stand to hear the Toronto fans cheering and so I would hit the "mute" button on my remote. Lo and behold, every time I did, a Toronto batter would make an out. Couldn't find the button that would produce any runs for the Orioles, however, who dropped two heart-breakers in the first two games of the series and had to settle for second. Even now, however, 35 years later, if the Orioles need an out, really need an out, I know what to do.

I bet Edward Lorenz, the guy who coined the term, "the butterfly effect" was a baseball fan.

This is all just superstitious behavior (probably). Any sane Chicagoan, for example, knows that goats and black cats did not keep the Cubs from the World Series for 71 years. Reason says that wearing the same Cubs hat and sweatshirt and engaging in a "ritual handshake" before each game has no influence on the outcome whatsoever. Reason also says, however, that by sheer chance, the Cubs should have been in the World Series at least once in the 71 seasons between 1945 and 2015. The Braves have been to the World Series eight times since 1945 representing *three different cities!* The trouble is that reason clearly does not rule the world or it would indeed be a sane place. Even as the Cubs were taking on the San Francisco Giants in the 2016 National League Divisional Series, an article by David Noonan appeared in *Scientific American* explaining that when reason fails us, we turn to our intuition to combat the unreasonable.[33] And so, 66 year-old season-ticket holder Michael Pardys, dons his Cubs hat and sweatshirt and does the handshake with his wife in an effort to influence the outcome of the game. Pardys was quoted as saying, "I feel really silly saying this, but I somehow feel the whole thing is really delicately balanced, that anything can change it." Naturally, as Noonan points out, seeing other people donning their lucky sweatshirts and caps reinforces the idea that maybe you're not crazy after all; that there really is something to it and it's just a matter of discovering the *right* handshake that will influence the chance that the Cubs will indeed, win the World Series.

Yet, just the night before, with the Cubs trailing the Giants 5-2 heading into the ninth inning, I am fairly certain that 99% of all Cubs fans were thinking the same thing: *Here we go again!* The Cubs had jumped out to a two games to none lead over the Giants just as they had in 1984 against the San Diego Padres who came back to win three straight and go to the World Series. They had jumped out to a three games to one lead in 2003 before losing three straight again, this time to the eventual World Series Champion Florida Marlins. That was the series, of course, in which Steve Bartman "interfered" with Moises Alou as the latter attempted to catch a foul ball along the left field stands in the seventh inning of the sixth game. The Cubs lost that game, lost the seventh game, and the curse continued and 99% of all Cub fans thought that the curse was about to continue against San Francisco, too. Surely, the Cubs would lose this game and then lose the fifth and deciding game. A glorious 103-win season would all be for naught and it would be another long winter and an anxious spring and an interminable summer just trying to get back to this same spot next season when a better handshake and a luckier hat would produce better results.

Something strange happened, though. Somehow, the Cubs employed some kind anti-curse, for it was *they* who scored four times in that ninth inning to defeat the Giants 6-5. And 99% of all Cubs fans know that the Giants shaky (I'm being kind; *inept* would be a better word) bullpen was only part of the reason for the victory.[34] Collectively, they had worn the right combination of lucky hats and socks and they made magic happen.

This exciting victory eliminated the Giants whose fans were expecting them to win the World Series because they had won it all in 2010, 2012, and 2014 so, *of course*, Fate or Math or Something said that since it was another even year, then the Giants were due to win again. An interesting theory arose among Giants fans when they discovered that singer Taylor Swift had released albums in 2010, 2012, and 2014, but not 2016. Obviously then, San Francisco's early exit from the 2016 playoff reveals that even-years were coincidental to, and not a cause of the Giants World Series success. The cause of San Francisco's failure in 2016 (and one assumes in 2011, 2013, and 2015) was clearly Taylor Swift.[35]

In the National League Championship Series, the Cubs won the first game, but then lost two straight to the Los Angeles Dodgers and again, a resigned fatalism descended upon Cub fans. Except, that the Cubs found their bats and won three straight to advance to the World Series. The morning after Chicago clinched, I read the following post on my Facebook feed from Lizzy Kipps of New Market, Virginia, a baseball lover and dedicated Cubs fan: "I woke up this morning and found out that apparently last night really happened. I wasn't dreaming. So now I'm going to cry some more."

There was certainly more than one Cubs fan crying at Wrigley Field that night, but the old familiar fatalism returned when the Cubs found themselves down three games to one to the American League champion Cleveland Indians. The North Siders won twice, however, to knot the Series at six games apiece and bring about Game Seven. With ever-rising hopes within the hearts of Cubs fans everywhere, Chicago led 5-1 heading to the bottom of the fifth and 6-3 with two outs in the 8th. I have no doubt when Tribe third baseman Jose Ramirez reached on an infield single that true Cub fans were overcome by a historic dread, which only increased when Brandon Guyer doubled home Ramirez to bring the tie-run to the plate in the person of Rajai Davis.

So when Ramirez reached and Guyer did the same, a sickly silence fell upon Cub patrons of the game.

Davis, who so far in the Series was three for twenty, stepped in against Aroldis Chapman, he of the fastest pitch ever recorded in major league history at 105 miles per hour. So, *of course*, the guy hitting .150 would homer off the guy with the liveliest arm in the big leagues. If I were a Cubs fan, I would have been screaming "I knew it!" through angry tears the moment Davis' line drive cleared the left field wall and hit the Fox Sports camera. And then I would have thrown my remote control at the television right before attempting to strangle myself.

After nine innings, the game was tied and to add to the misery of the moment, it began to rain. Somewhere in Cubville during that 17 minute delay, however, someone did the lucky handshake while wearing her lucky sweatshirt while turning her hat into a rally cap or she did Something, because the Cubs went out and promptly scored two runs in the top of the tenth. Even then; even after 108 years, even after the goat and the black cat and the collapse in 1984 and the collapse in 2003 and falling behind three games to one and Rajai Davis' home run and falling to score Jason Heyward from third with one out in the top of the ninth, even then there was one more agonizing, terrifying moment. With two outs *two outs!* Cub pitcher Carl Edwards, Jr. walked Brandon Guyer, thus bringing the tie-run to the plate once again. That meant Rajai Davis was approaching the batter's box. Davis, whose eighth inning home run had upped his average in the Series to .190, singled in Guyer who had advanced to second on defensive indifference and now the winning run *the winning run!* stepped to the plate. But something magical happened once more: Michael Martinez grounded out. The game was over. The Chicago Cubs were the World Champions. Now Cub fans and players were crying. We'll never know whose lucky sweatshirt should be sent to Cooperstown, but we do know that this marvelous, magical World Series victory meant a great deal to a great many. Chicago police estimated that five million people turned out for the Cubs Victory Parade two days after the clincher in Cleveland. Thus, that parade marks the seventh largest gathering in *human history*.[36]

My scientifically bent friends would scoff at a baseball gene much less magic of any kind, so maybe my passion for the game is an archetype that for some reason plays more forcefully in the core of us baseball people than it does in most others'. Maybe baseball is a modern version of one of Carl Jung's primitive archetypes. (Of course, there was a Daniel Jung who played 83 games at shortstop in the Rio Grande Valley League in 1950. Hit only .219 and made a whopping 66 errors, so it's no wonder he only lasted one year. No matter. I would have much rather had Daniel Jung's one poor season down in Texas, than Carl Jung's career. Besides, Carl probably would have made 77 errors.)

Psychology majors will immediately argue that an archetype must develop over thousands of years; that it arises as part of the human evolutionary process. I would argue that if there is no baseball archetype per se, the game certainly encapsulates several of the most basic, and, therefore, several of our most resonate archetypes.

The hero archetype is an obvious one, but then all the other sports have heroes as well. The baseball park itself, also represents an archetype, in this case we might call it an agricultural archetype. Many, *many*, baseball fans cherish the memory of the first time they ascended the ramp from a ballpark's concourse to the grandstand to be greeted by the thrill of seeing all that green grass. Indeed, W. P, Kinsella, author of *Shoeless Joe* the book on which the movie *Field of Dreams* was based wrote a short story entitled, "The Thrill of the Grass." Football stadiums contain just as much grass, however, if not more.

The explanation for the thrill of the baseball grass seems to lie in the fact that it is arranged according to an agricultural sensibility. The dirt infield is a contrast to the grassy outfield and these terms were used, especially in Scottish farming as far back as the 17th century. The former was, and still is a cultivated field closest to the farmstead. The latter is uncultivated; it is pasture. Indeed, baseball's Creation Myth, i.e. that Abner Doubleday invented the game on Phinney's Lot in Cooperstown, New York hearkens to this very idea, and the image of knickers-clad boys running about small-town America developing in their own innocent way the National Pastime is almost sacred. (The reality, of course is that the game was developed in the Eastern cities, primarily Brooklyn.)

Again, psychology majors, led by the no-hit, no-field Carl Jung might argue that even agriculture is too modern a phenomenon to have become an archetype, but I would contend that the "agricultural archetype" is simply a refined version of the savannah archetype. In their 1997 work, *Painting by Numbers: Komar and Melamid's Scientific Guide to Art*, Vitaly Komar and Alex Melamid commissioned pollsters to determine what kind of painting the average person most liked. The universal answer was "the kind of natural environment in which humans evolved. There is wide agreement among biological anthropologists that this environment was the savannah of east Africa," a land basically, flat and green, but with some irregularities such as clumps of trees.[37] Almost as sacred to baseball fans as the grass are the irregularities of baseball parks. Fenway Park has the Green Monster and AT&T Park in San Francisco has all kinds of corners and quirks, for example. Coors Field in Denver actually has trees and rocks and a pond beyond the center field fence. So, too, does Angel Stadium of Anaheim. Kauffman Stadium in Kansas City has a water feature as well. Minute Maid Park actually put a rise in play with a small hill in center field before removing it after the 2016 season. Football stadiums may be historic, but they are not quirky. The same football field could be installed in any football stadium; after all, they are gridirons, with an emphasis on the *grid*. They all look the same, with the exception of the blue turf at Boise State, which conjures the image of one of those 1964 color TVs on the fritz.

Entering a baseball park (emphasis on *park*) seems to set off signals in the most primitive parts of our brains that says, "This is a good place to be."

We not only feel anchored to the Earth when at a game, we are also afforded a glimpse of the Infinite. Many, *many* baseball fans routinely come away from a game saying, "I've never seen that before!" in reference to some play. Consider that on any given pitch there are, by my count, 37 different possible outcomes: a ball, strike, foul or HBP; five different hits including a bunt hit; nine fair fly outs, eight foul fly outs, six ground outs, and five bunt outs. (I'm omitting such esoteric possibilities as cannon-armed right fielder throwing out a slow runner at first base.) My aforementioned buddy Al spent 30 years as a weapons systems analyst for the Department of the Army. Math was involved. Lots of math, and so I asked him if one could even calculate the odds that the exact sequence of any two baseball games would ever repeat themselves. His answer: "I can say with 100% confidence that the probability of your event occurring is nonzero. However as t (time) approaches infinity the answer (limit of the function) is zero. I hope this sheds some light on the problem." I'm still in the dark, but translated, Al's answer is an empathic *No!*

I suppose that every football or basketball game has been unique as well, but somehow there is just no vibe of the Infinite at those contests, perhaps because, as Earl Weaver famously said, "You can't sit on a lead and run a few plays into the line and just kill the clock. You've got to throw the ball over the damn plate and give the other man his chance. That's why baseball is the greatest game of them all." It's hard to argue with one of baseball's greatest arguers.

Baseball provides not only a glimpse of the Infinite, but also a glimpse of the Eternal. The great irony of baseball is that because time is meaningless to the game, it restores Time to those who play and watch. What is Time anyway, but the moment in which you exist? And if you have "now" you have all the time in the world. Baseball is not divided into linear chunks of time during which some event occurs. It is a series of moments, some that seem agonizingly long, others tantalizingly short . . . the pitcher stares in for a sign, shakes once, then nods. The batter waves his bat awaiting the delivery. The pitcher rocks and delivers . . . The great radio play-by-play men are great because they talk not about WAR and WHIP or even batting averages and ERAs; they describe the moments of the game.[38] Furthermore, if the pitcher shakes off untold signs there is no delay-of-game penalty. The timelessness of baseball gives you time; time to talk to the guy in the next seat, time to guess what pitch is coming, time for a hot dog, time to take in the full moon rising above the park, time to glance at your child and remember when your father took you. The game almost *makes* you be mindful of the moment. To be mindful is to slow down, to embrace the here and now, to rid oneself of anxiety over the past that we can't change and the future that we don't know.

It is interesting to note that "mindfulness" is a Buddhist practice embraced in the United States by the 19th century Transcendentalists, including Walt Whitman, who, of course, was a big baseball fan. As of this writing (November, 2016) there is even a website out there called *Zen Baseball: A Non-expert Exploring the Intersection of Baseball and Mindfulness*. (http://zenbaseball.tumblr.com/) Makes you wonder if Thich Nhat Hanh is a baseball fan.[39]

Indeed, if you Google "God + baseball" you may be amazed at the number of very serious books that have been written on the subject. There's *God and Baseball*, by J. H. Sauls; *Crossing Home: The Spiritual Lessons of Baseball*, by James Penrice; and a 2013 work by New York University President James Sexton entitled, *Baseball As a Road to God: Seeing Beyond the Game* to name three.

Anthropologists and psychologists and sociologists and probably even the mixologist at your local tavern all agree that religion is a universal phenomenon because it is an evolutionary adaptation. While individual and cultural rituals and conceptions of God may vary, the core of religion's universality is faith. We believe for the same reasons that we eat and breathe, i.e. because we're humans and we must do so in order to survive. Ya gotta believe.

Because of its structure, baseball is a game of faith. If your football team is trailing by four touchdowns with a minute left in the game, your team is not going to win. Period. If your baseball team is trailing by four runs with two down in the bottom of the 9th, you still have a chance. If your baseball team is trailing by *fourteen* runs with two down in the bottom of the 9th, you still have a chance. Such comebacks happen just often enough to reward our faith. Every now and then, Brooks Robinson really DOES deliver a ninth inning hit to win the game. Every now and then, a team such as the 1973 New York Mets, who were ten games under .500 at the end of August come back and win their division. As every baseball fan knows, Tug McGraw, a relief pitcher for those Mets kept telling his teammates and the fans "Ya gotta believe!" Their faith was rewarded with the National League pennant. The Mets, believing in great marketing when they saw it, trademarked the slogan. The Mets' marketing move should not be greeted with cynicism, however. The United Methodist Church, for example, has trademarked its cross and flame symbol and the website for the General Council on Finance and Administration notes that "if you are interested in purchasing Cross and Flame products for your church or personal use (e.g. church signs, mugs, stationery) from officially licensed vendors" then you may contact one of their stores.[40]

I'm not singling out the Methodists for particular criticism. I just happen to be more familiar with them having been raised a Methodist and having earned a Master of Theological Studies degree from Wesley Theological Seminary in Washington, D. C. Indeed, my grandfather became a Methodist minister. (My education didn't provide any special insight into faith, but I do know more of the big words in religion textbooks than the average person.)

It's not the reward of faith, however, that stokes the passion of baseball people. It is the *exercise* of faith. That explains those long-suffering Chicago Cub fans.

This exercise of faith is, I think, the genesis for my passion for the game, and I suspect that it explains the passion of most baseball people.

John Thorn, Major League Baseball's Official Historian, put it this way in a June 16, 2011 entry to his *Our Game* blog, entitled, appropriately enough, "Ya Gotta Believe":

Rooting is all about vicarious experience, surrogacy, sublimation, and emulation. When we cheer for our favorites or implore them to win we are doing many other things as well: reenacting archaic rites, reliving past glories, transferring powers from our heroes to ourselves and, by emulating warfare rather than engaging in it, ensuring the future of the world. In sharing an experience that, like faith, insists upon no generational divide, boys learn what it is like to be men and men recall what it was like to be boys. The ballpark, even when visited through electronic media, forms a magic circle in which all this metaphysical swirl underlies not a staged drama or religious rite, with their preordained outcomes, but a real life struggle in which risk is everywhere present.[41]

The spiritual appeal of baseball is not just that it provides a doorway to the Infinite and Eternal. It's not just the sacred green spaces in which it is played nor the ancestors which it conjures. Baseball, unlike most religions is both dynamic and democratic. The deities and the sacred numbers and the cathedrals are never forgotten, but they do constantly evolve, and each generation may claim its own. Luis Aparicio became Mark Belanger who became Cal Ripken at shortstop for the Orioles. Two-thousand, one hundred and thirty straight games became 2,632. Memorial Stadium became Camden Yards. Every fan, be it man, woman, or child is his own priest, free to worship Cal Ripken or Kiko Garcia, free to determine that the foul ball caught off the bat of Curt Motten in a game otherwise long-forgotten is indeed a sacred relic, free to create his own rituals be it wearing lucky socks or pressing the mute button whenever an out is needed.

I suspect, too, that it is this dynamic and democratic nature of the game that appeals to those who play it at all levels. Rick Dempsey, for example, began his professional career in 1967 when he was drafted in the 15th round of that year's amateur draft. He reached the big leagues in 1969 at age 20, played in four different decades, and finally retired in 1992 at age 43. Since then he has served as a minor league coach and manager, a major league coach, and a broadcaster. He has yet to see it all. When Dempsey was introduced at the Orioles 60th Anniversary celebration after the game on August 8, 2014, he waved to the fans, walked to the plate, got down on one knee, and kissed it.

You pick up a ball and nestle it in your fingertips. It is connected to your hand and by extension to your elbow and shoulder. You can't recall the first time you picked one up, because that memory resides somewhere in the muscles, but in the moment of bringing your arm forward and sending that ball on its way, you exist simultaneously in a multitude of moments, including the first one when you were two and you could throw it across your entire world.

3 REDEMPTION

The only thing that kept me from fulfilling my Destiny of replacing Brooks Robinson at third base for the Orioles was a lack of talent. It took me 35 years to forgive myself for not being a better baseball player.

When I was 12, no less an authority than Butch Jones's dad, who coached a team in the Carroll Manor Recreation League, said that I would be a big leaguer. What more confirmation did I need? It was a foolish and irresponsible thing to say about a 12-year old and I would probably have adjusted better to my ultimate failure as a ballplayer if it had never been said. Yet, I still feel the glee that those words engendered, and in some ways, the knowledge that one person at one time thought I had big league talent is *still* the greatest compliment I've ever received. I *know* that's not true, but my inner 12-year old has a hard time letting that go.

I believed in Destiny more than hard work, which I didn't know anything about anyway. There were no clinics in those days and no indoor batting cages. You didn't go to Dick's Sporting Goods and buy a bucket of balls for the summer; you went to Montgomery Wards and got one new ball, brilliant in its whiteness that you saved for special occasions. For all other occasions you used last year's ball, assuming that it hadn't been lost in the neighbor's hedge or gotten water-logged by too many foul balls into the creek. Last year's ball was not white, but rather a solid brown with a green hue that had been sealed by the dog running around the yard carrying it in his mouth.

I did do a few things to prepare for what I thought was my future. Every 8th grader in the academic track at Ridgley Junior High School had to sign up for a language. Naturally, I took Spanish, and when asked on the first day of class, why we signed up for the language that we did I wrote on the index card, "In order to speak to my Latin American teammates when I reach the major leagues."

Up to about 12 I was big for my age and my father calculated that I would be about 6'2" and maybe 180 pounds. Those sounded like good numbers for the back of my baseball card, but as it turned out, he was off by four inches and forty pounds. By high school, the other boys had caught up to me in size and coordination. I played two years of varsity baseball and one year of American Legion ball. I tried out for my Division III college team my freshman year and, winters what they are in Maryland, we worked out in the gym quite often. I had had trouble throwing the baseball in my junior year of high school, probably a mechanical issue, but with my Destiny abandoning me, I feared making a mistake of any kind, lest it leave me all together. I was a nervous wreck on every throw especially since we were playing almost shoulder to shoulder in that gym. There was no room for error, but I made plenty. Ultimately, I made the taxi squad, catching one fly ball and garnering two at-bats, all in the same game. That was the end of my playing career.

The throwing problems stayed with me. I sweated throwing batting practice when I coached Becky's Little League team and if Al would visit and want to play catch, I sweated that, too. Somehow, I was afraid to do something that I loved dearly. Watching Rick Ankiel fall apart on the mound during the 2000 postseason was personally heartbreaking.[42] One day in 2011, after playing and sweating out a game of catch with friends, I had had enough and actually sought professional help. I wanted to bring back the joy. Working with a brainspotting therapist, I "went within." I was able to overcome the malady and one important component was learning to forgive myself. After all, baseball IS a game of failure.

According to numbers cited in a 2005 article by Steven D. Keener, the President and Chief Executive Officer of Little League International, of the 5,000,000 kids who play baseball, 400,000 will play for their high school team.[43] That's 8%. Parkville American Legion, for whom I played, drew from four different high schools, which by applying math and drawing a rough parallel means that I made it further in my baseball career than 98% of all those other eight-year olds who ever graced a Little League field. Keener estimates that of the 400,000 high school players, 1,500 are signed to professional contracts. Rounding up that's .04%. Keener also estimates that of those 1,500 professionals only 100 reach the majors where the average career is 5.6 years.[44] As of the first week of the 2015 season there have been 16,203 major league baseball players since the American League was formed in 1901 and there are 215 players in the Hall of Fame or 1.3%.[45]

You just might make the Hall of Fame if you accumulate a .300 lifetime average or win 300 games, and your career lasts at least 10 years, the minimum number of seasons for eligibility. Even once you make the Hall of Fame, it might very well be the failures that you remember. Writing in his autobiography 23 years after the fact, Ted Williams described his disappointment at hitting .200 in the 1946 World Series. In Game Seven, which Williams' Red Sox would lose 4-3 to the Cardinals, he hit two flies that almost went out of the park, but of course, "almost" never counts. "I was just so disgusted, so unhappy, and I couldn't believe we lost," he wrote in his autobiography, *My Turn at Bat: The Story of My Life*. "I was shell-shocked. I was so disappointed in myself. Just sick inside."[46] Williams anguish is alive yet on the page. He gave his World Series money to the clubhouse man.

Or as Manager Jimmy Dugan tells Dottie Hinson in *A League of Their Own*, "The hard is what makes it great." Dottie, the star catcher for the Rockford Peaches who was always somewhat reticent about playing, has decided to leave the team and go home. "It's just a game," she blasphemes to Jimmy. Dugan understands this attitude, however, having thrown away five years of his career on drinking. "And now there isn't anything I wouldn't give to get back one day of it," he tells her. This doesn't seem to register with Dottie, however, and in disgust Dugan turns to leave, but he knows Dottie better than she knows herself and tells her to look within. "Baseball is what gets inside you," he hisses at her. "It's what lights you up. You can't deny that." When Dottie replies that "It just got too hard," Dugan tells her, "It's supposed to be hard. If it wasn't hard everyone would do it. The hard is what makes it great."

Five million Little Leaguers, 215 Hall of Famers.

I knew all those numbers about how so few of us become professional ballplayers years ago, but it is hard to give up a dream. This is, of course, in spite of all the evidence that suggested, no demanded, that I acknowledge the facts of the case. Make that *the fact* of the case: I didn't have the talent. Adults, however, are the ones who weigh evidence and draw conclusions. When I was a child, I thought as a child, but our development is not linear it is cumulative. This meant that there was still a pre-pubescent voice inside me that kept saying, "But Butch Jones's father said . . ."

It was time for a meeting of the minds which is to say all the minds that exist inside my brain. I cannot say why this meeting took place at the age of 53 and not 33; it doesn't matter. Once I was able to explain to the 12-year old that *we* are not going to make it rather than *he* wasn't going to make it, he was able to let go of the dream and devote *his* energy to *my* dreams. We agreed that I didn't fail at baseball, I just wasn't good enough to play beyond the level that I did. What a basic concept! What a simple, liberating concept! Not even a Hall of Famer can play beyond the level of his ability. Opening a pack of baseball cards and seeing myself in the stack was a beautiful dream and it remains so, but it is itself a relic of youth and now, so consigned. The dreamer of that dream is currently busy helping me with other stuff.

I guess I had it easy, though. Ray Kinsella had to plow under his corn, build a baseball field, kidnap Terrance Mann, find Moonlight Graham, and almost lose his farm before he found redemption. In the process, however, he also delivered redemption to his brother-in-law Mark who suddenly saw the Magic; to Terrance Mann, whose cynicism was washed away and he walked into the cornfield to explore the Magic; and especially to Shoeless Joe Jackson.

Jackson's fall from grace as a member of the 1919 Chicago Black Sox is still a source of fascination precisely because his story is universal. Joe Jackson was an affable, illiterate country boy from the wilds of South Carolina who yielded to the temptation of gamblers' money. Well, maybe he did. Some say that he never took a bribe to throw the 1919 World Series to the Cincinnati Reds; some say that he didn't know what he was doing because he was such an innocent; and some say that he agreed to participate in the fix, then regretted it and played hard, trying to redeem the dirty Sox and lead Chicago to a championship. All cite the fact that his .375 average led the Series that year and his six runs batted in were tops on the White Sox.

Nevertheless, Shoeless Joe, was banned for life from organized baseball by Judge Kennesaw Mountain Landis who reasoned that even if Joe didn't take any money, he should have told someone that his shady teammates had.

We've all been in Joe Jackson's shoes, even if he didn't wear any, whether we did something that we regretted or did something that we didn't realize was a terrible mistake at the time or were simply punished excessively or unfairly for an innocent mistake or even no mistake at all. There's the legendary story of the boy on the courthouse steps who, upon hearing that Jackson was guilty, plaintively called out, "Say it ain't so, Joe!" to which the saddened ballplayer could only reply, "Yes, kid, I'm afraid it is."

The factuality of this part of the story has been argued endlessly since the day that Joe exited the courthouse. Which would be September 28, 1920 to be precise, but neither the date nor the identity of this broken-hearted kid really matters. He exists without doubt. He exists inside of every person who has ever had his or her innocence stripped away in one fell swoop or whoever realized that he wasn't good enough to play professionally or whoever realized that his heroes were mortal after all. Our heroes or our parents. We can wish that it ain't so, but it is: Our teams lose, our heroes strike out, our favorite players get old, retire, die. It becomes impossible to remain a boy awash in innocence. Baseball can be a game of failure on the inside as well as on the field.

Theologian Paul Tillich wrote about the nature of true faith versus idolatrous faith stating that in the former one's "ultimate concern" is about the Truly Ultimate, whereas the latter elevates finite realities to the level of the Ultimate. (Capitalization is mine.)[47] The Shoeless Joe from *Field of Dreams*, elevated winning above the Game; given a second chance, he realizes what he lost and is now grateful for what he has found, namely a ballfield in the middle of a cornfield in Iowa, at least according to the parable that is *Field of Dreams*. He will not find a place in the big leagues, but his place in the Universe has been redeemed.

"I'd have played for food money. I'd have played free and worked for food," says Jackson.[48]

And now Jackson and the other members of the Black Sox can play in Eternity on the diamond that Ray Kinsella built.

Field of Dreams is as much a spiritual movie as it is a baseball movie. Certainly, *Shoeless Joe* is a spiritual novel as there are over 25 specific religious allusions in a work that is 224 pages long which averages one every 10 pages or so.[49] Interestingly, an important character from the book, Eddie Scissions, never made it into the movie. If Ray is a prophet, and Terrance Mann (who is actually J. D. Salinger in the book) is the first disciple, and Shoeless Joe is a fallen angel, then Eddie Scissions represents the rest of us. Scissions, claims to be the last living member of the last (until this year) Chicago Cubs World Championship team from 1908. He is lying, however, which a quick check of the *Baseball Encyclopedia* reveals. Ray, however, does not call him out on this, and indeed, the players allow Scissions to take the mound during one of their games. Eddie Scissions sits in the bleachers watching "Kid" Scissions pitch. He discovers, much as I did, and the vast majority of us have, that he just didn't have the talent. The major leaguers from the cornfield light him up and he is relieved without retiring a batter.

Later, Ray asks him if he still believes in baseball. "It takes more than an infinite ERA to shake my faith," Eddie "chuckles not unhappily."[50]

He dies shortly thereafter, apparently after a premonition of death, for he is found lying on his bed in his Chicago Cubs uniform. He is buried in left-field, Shoeless Joe's position, and at Shoeless Joe's insistence. "He loved the game as much as anyone can," says Joe and all the players file past Eddie's open coffin, hats in hand.[51]

Kid Scissions had misplaced his faith in his talent, but not in the Game. Joe recognized that and made sure that the guy who in fact was not "the oldest living member of the 1908 Chicago Cubs" was honored for that unwavering faith.

Baseball lets you know if your faith is misplaced. Neither baseball nor life is about the final score, to repeat what Thomas Boswell wrote. Our teams lose, our heroes strike out, our favorite players get old, retire, die. Would anyone remember *Casey at the Bat* if the mighty slugger had knocked in Flynn and Blake? O. Henry once wrote, "Life is made up of sobs, sniffles, and smiles, with sniffles predominating"[52]

Becky and I experienced all three during one long night in Luray, Virginia. She and I had become fans of the New Market Rebels, a team in the Valley Baseball League, which is a college summer league. New Market is 90 miles from where we lived in Williamsport, Maryland, but there was something about the old ballpark in which the Rebels played, seeing the same fans at every game, the enthusiasm of these young players, and rooting together in Virginia's soft summer evenings that compelled us to make the drive. In 2004, the Rebels were in a deciding playoff game against their arch-rivals from across Massanutten Mountain, the Luray Wranglers and we had to be there, despite the fact that the game was in Luray and added another 20 miles to our trip.

The contest began on July 31st at 7:34 according to our scorecard, and it saw the Rebels jump out to a 5-2 lead after two innings. The game settled down until the 7th when Luray scored three to tie and they could have had more when Donnie Burkhalter lifted a fly ball to right with Brian Bocock on third. Bocock, however, had attempted to steal home on the pitch and by the time he got back to third it was too late to tag up. During the next at-bat, Daniel Murphy, who was on first, then ran half way to second hoping to get hung up long enough to allow Bocock to score, but was thrown out 2-4-3 before Bocock crossed the plate.[53] (This is the same Daniel Murphy who hit homers for the New York Mets in six straight playoff games in 2015 and finished second in the National League batting race in 2016 with a .347 mark.) To the delight of Rebel fans, New Market's catcher, Steve Smith, homered in the 8th and when Luray scored in the bottom half of the inning, the game was tied again.

As it turned out, the game was not quite half over.

Both teams put two runners on in the 11th, but failed to score. The Rebels had runners on first and third with one out in the 14th, but were kept off the board. Murphy led off the 15th with a double for the Wranglers, but was left stranded. It was now well past midnight and the fans who remained, which was most of us, in this tiny little ballpark that sits along U. S. 340 at the entrance to town, joked that the game was a month old. After all, it was now August 1st.

Both teams went three up, three down in the 16th as did the Rebels in the top of the 17th. After Murphy grounded out and Burkhalter struck out, Brandon Pope stepped to the plate and stroked a laser beam toward right field. I didn't think it was hit high enough to get out and neither did right fielder, Marion Knowles who turned to play the carom off the wall. The carom never came. The ball sailed over the fence and into the darkness of the Virginia night. The end was stunningly sudden.

Becky cried the all the way back over the mountain. "It's not fair!"

Recently, however, I asked her about her favorite baseball memory that the two of us ever shared. "That game against Luray," was her immediate reply. "The fun we had rooting with everybody; that we were all in it together. . . . That was my favorite memory even though we lost."

"*Even though we lost.*" This bitter defeat had been turned to a golden thread in the fabric of her faith.

Indeed, Tillich reminds us that faith is not a guarantee of anything and that "living faith includes the doubt about itself, the courage to take this doubt into itself, and the risk of courage."[54]

That's why we admire Mighty Casey even though he struck out. He put himself on the line and tested his faith in himself. He dared to fail. After all, the pitcher who put the third strike past Casey isn't even mentioned.

Faith is separate from belief, which is derived from a series of calculations. Becky and I believed that we were going to win that game against Luray, which was actually a reasonable assumption. I believed that Paul Blair was going to hit that home run in 1966. That was a far less reasonable assumption, but it came true. Nevertheless, those calculations, however improbable, may produce a sense of magic, and a sense of the Magical opens the door to a Universe that is beyond reason, beyond comprehension, one which can only be referred to metaphorically.

Baseball is the perfect metaphor. Just ask O. Henry:

"All of life, as we know it, moves in little, unavailing circles. More justly than to anything else, it can be likened to the game of baseball. Crack! We hit the ball, and away we go. If we earn a run (in life we call it success) we get back to the home plate and sit upon a bench. If we are thrown out, we walk back to the home plate -- and sit upon a bench."

4 WHERE TWO OR MORE ARE GATHERED

When I was in third grade in the spring of 1966, my Sunday school teacher, and next door neighbor, Mr. Wade had all of his students memorize the 23rd Psalm. He gave out various little trinkets as a reward to each of us when we successfully recited the psalm. I received a baseball.

Perhaps five or six years later, Mr. Wade saw me in the yard one day and asked if I'd like to go to the Orioles game at Memorial Stadium that night. Always comfortable around adults, this was one of the first times I remember *feeling* like an adult. Here we were, just two guys, one of whom would be happily unencumbered by parents, heading out to a game. What bridged the 55 years or so that separated us was a common language. We both spoke baseball.

The common language of baseball creates an instant community wherever two or more speakers are gathered.

Just the day before I began to write this chapter, I received a call from Maynard G. "Mo" Weber, a dear friend, under whom I did my graduate work in baseball and who taught me more about the game in the last few years than I had learned in the first 50. Mo was born on June 22, 1923 which puts him at 93 as of this writing. After serving as an infantryman in World War II, Mo went to Winona State Teachers College (now Winona State University) in Minnesota where he began his coaching career in 1946. He hung up the uniform for good after the

2011 season, which means that he had coached baseball in one form or another from the Truman administration down to the Obama administration. Mo's health is failing and he no longer has the energy to come out at 4:00 p.m. to watch his hitters take batting practice, then assist managers young enough to be his grandsons, then talk about the game just played while eating the post-game meal, and then keep talking about the game just played until 2:00 a.m. This was our routine when he coached and I did play-by-play on the webcasts for the New Market Rebels.[55] Among other topics that Mo covered during our phone call was the positioning of the third baseman on the bag when a throw is coming in from right field as opposed to left field. (Stay on the inside of the base when taking a throw from right and on the outside when taking a throw from left. Never straddle the base so as not to get your legs tangled with the baserunner's.) I commented that the chance that a throw would be right to the bag, even in the major leagues was probably only 30% and much less at the college level. Mo readily concurred, then added, "You and I speak the same language."

Half the time, that language doesn't even include "Hello!" at least not when Mo's on the other end of the line. Earlier in the year we had attended a Rebels game together. The next day, my phone rang and I saw who was calling.

"Hi, Mo!"

"What in the world are we doing trying to steal third base with two out?"

"Hello!" wasn't really necessary anyway.

***

It's that ability to speak baseball that not only connects us to a single, fellow fan, but to a fellowship at large. That was one of the things Becky remembered most about that 17 inning game against Luray. I remember experiencing this fellowship at a young age at Memorial Stadium whenever we would sit near a group of cigar-smoking men— yes, people used to do such things in public—who would talk baseball through the entire game.

"Aparicio is going to steal, you watch!"

"Nope, I gotta take Mays over Mantle."

"How can you swing at that pitch on 2-0?"

I listened and I learned and even now the smell of cigar smoke takes me back to my childhood days at the ballpark.

Of course, there were times that I got to actively participate in the services. The aforementioned Aparicio, i.e. Luis, the American League stolen base champ from 1956-1964, played five seasons for the Orioles and I was awed the first time Memorial Stadium broke into a chant of "Go! Go! Go!" exhorting Little Luis to take off for second. Someone not versed in the language might have wondered *who* was supposed to go, and *where* and why 30,000 of us were all shouting it at the same time. I'm not sure if such information is really translatable. Oh, you could explain what was going on, but if you don't speak baseball, you're just not going to get the real meaning even if you eventually understand the facts.[56]

Baseball people are all members of the same faith at least for nine innings. We all know the words to the one hymn, "Take Me Out to the Ballgame," that will be sung during the Passing of the Peace which is otherwise known as the seventh inning stretch. Interestingly, I have found this to be true whether I am attending my home "church" or one to which I have never been before.

In July of 2015, Al and I took a long-anticipated trip to the Hillerich & Bradsby Factory and Museum in Louisville, Kentucky and then drove up to Indiana where we wanted to visit two particular ballparks: League Stadium in Huntingburg and Bosse Field in Evansville. Huntingburg is the home of the Dubois County Bombers, a collegiate summer league team in the Ohio Valley League.

The Bombers play at League Stadium, which is where much of *A League of Their Own* was filmed, serving as the home field of the movie's Rockford Peaches. League Stadium was left to the people of Huntingburg in all its glorious 1940s ballpark fashion by Columbia Pictures and I wanted to shoot a video there for a YouTube series entitled, *Off the Beaten Basepaths* about little known baseball sites.

I emailed ahead to make sure that I had permission to do so. Mary Uebelhor, whose husband Mike is the Managing Partner of the Bombers, was most gracious in her response, not only granting permission, but giving us an open invitation to explore the ballpark and talk to anyone around, including any of "the Peaches." These are the young ladies who take tickets, paint eye black on younger fans (older fans, too, no doubt, but I didn't think to ask), and provide between-innings entertainment while wearing replica uniforms of the original Rockford Peaches. Mary is one of those hard-working, behind-the-scenes volunteers that make hundreds of such teams hum throughout the summer. Mary's job title, however, is a bit less formal than Mike's.

"I manage the managing partner, but he doesn't always take my managing!" she said.

Mary took time from her busy pre-game schedule to make sure that we were taken care of and Mike did the same, talking to us at length about college summer baseball. We all spoke the same language and because Al and I were already involved with the New Market Rebels, it was as if we spoke the same dialect. By game time, we were no longer strangers. By the time it concluded (a wild 13-6 loss by the Bombers who would nevertheless win their first OVL championship in the next two weeks) we were friends.

The next night we attended a Frontier League (independent) game between the Evansville Otters and the Joliet Slammers at historic Bosse Field in Evansville. Bosse opened on June 17, 1915 making it the third oldest professional ballpark in the country behind Fenway Park (1912) and Wrigley Field (1914). Bosse also served as the "away" ballpark in *A League of Their Own*. Al and I treated ourselves to seats right behind the Otters' dugout which naturally aroused the curiosity of those folks who routinely sit behind the Otters' dugout. The fact that we were there on a night when the heat index registered 100 at game time was a good indication that we were indeed baseball people and were not merely misplaced tourists. After we started talking with one another, we became instant locals. We talked at length to Dave Meyer, a teacher and athletic director. Behind him sat his daughter, Erin, with his father, Jim. After talking baseball for a while, Dave became eager to have us meet Bix Branson, the Otters' General Manager and he introduced us as a couple of "real baseball guys," which is a high compliment indeed. Bix bade us come with him to his office where he handed us some souvenir tickets from Bosse Field's Centennial Game and proudly showed us a photo hanging on the office wall of that June day, one hundred years ago when the ballpark opened.

I doubt that Bix Branson or Dave Meyer or anyone else in Bosse Field the night we visited could have named anyone in that photo of the inaugural game, but we would have been right at home sitting next to any one of those early baseball fans, and they with us, because we not only shared the same language, but the same faith, which explains why I have kept in touch with Mary and Dave.

Common beliefs beget communities and communities require a public space in which to gather and reaffirm those common beliefs. The public space itself becomes sacred after a time because we not only come to this place to worship now, but so did our ancestors. Hence the reverence baseball people hold for ballparks or in some cases, the space where the ballpark once stood.

David Stinson, a former Department of Justice lawyer, turned author has made a hobby of visiting the sites where old ballparks once stood. He has visited dozens of such sites from New York to Florida to Arizona and details each pilgrimage on his website, deadballbaseball.com Indeed, his novel *Deadball: A Metaphysical Baseball Novel* tells the tale of one Byron Bennett, a fictional minor league ballplayer who sees ghosts, not only of old ballplayers, but also of the parks in which they played. Byron has glimpses of Forbes Field, Baltimore's Union Park, the home of John McGraw's pennant–winning Orioles of the 1890s, and League Park in Cleveland.

League Park has been "repurposed" to use the modern lexicon, and youth baseball fields complete with artificial turf now cover the acreage. When Stinson visited in 2009, however, it was still simply an abandoned ballpark site. While exploring the grounds, he discovered sheets of plywood on the ground, which as it turned out, were covering the in-ground portion of the dugouts.

"I wanted to get a picture of that dugout," relates Stinson, "and so I lowered my then 9 year-old son down into the pit. He took my camera and he started taking pictures of everything. You couldn't believe it. The paint is still on the walls. This is where all these great ballplayers walked to and from the clubhouse. It's all still there, just covered by plywood. And it wasn't that long ago."

Even the razing of Yankee Stadium agitated Stinson, who as an Oriole fan, quite naturally despises the team that began its life in American League Park, also known as Oriole Park IV,[57] as the original American League Baltimore franchise.

"When they started tearing down Yankee Stadium, I was bothered by that. Even though I can't stand the Yankees, I can respect them as a team and their history and I can respect Yankee Stadium itself. I can't believe they tore it down. But they did and so I, a die-hard Oriole fan, felt compelled to purchase pieces of the old ballpark."

These relics include three different signs, a piece of the outfield wall, and a brick.

Stinson did not attend many games as a youngster, but in his budding adulthood, he went to games at The Vet in Philadelphia and at Wrigley Field and he began to enjoy the experience of "collecting ballparks." One of those few early games, however, was pivotal.

"When I was a teenager, my dad took me to Memorial Stadium which was probably the most important game I ever went to because my dad took me. He said, 'What do you want for your birthday?' I said, 'I want you, my dad, to take me to a baseball game because that's what dads do." Father and son picked this particular game because the California Angels were in town and Frank Robinson, David's favorite player, was now DHing for the Angels after having been traded to California by the Dodgers during the off-season. This was his first chance to see the future Hall of Famer now that he was back in the American League after having played six glorious years for the Orioles. The pitching match-up that day, May 6, 1973 also happened to feature Nolan Ryan versus Jim Palmer in a game the Orioles won 5-0.

The experience of being in the ballpark with his dad resonated with such meaning, that, once Stinson became a father himself, he felt compelled to take his own children to the ballpark, or perhaps more accurately, to as many ballparks as possible.

When my daughter was born in '91, it was the last year of the Orioles in Memorial Stadium, and it became my thing: I had to take her to Memorial Stadium to see a game before they tore it down. And so I took her. We sat in the bleachers. I got all these pictures of her and it lit something inside me that had been dormant for many years and that was my love of baseball. It became this drive in me that I wanted to take my kids to ballgames and not just to Camden Yards or to minor league ballparks but around the country. So I put them in the car and started chasing ballparks. I wanted them to have the ability to say, "Yeah, I saw a ballgame at Camden Yards; I saw a game at Memorial Stadium." And so when my son Calvin was 9 years-old, I took him to Tiger Stadium because I wanted him to be able to say, I saw a game at Tiger Stadium. And that's what spawned my love of the cathedrals.

Stinson is far from the only person who loves "the cathedrals." In some cases, even the site upon which a cathedral once stood beckons the fellowship. In Pittsburgh, Forbes Field, was home to the Pirates from 1909 through the middle of the 1970 season. It was also the scene of the only walk off, World Series Game Seven home run, which was hit by Bill Mazeroski in the bottom of the 9th in 1960. The site, which had already been purchased by the University of Pittsburgh and rented back to the Pirates was finally taken over by the school in 1971 when the Pirates moved into Three Rivers Stadium. Posvar Hall now sits atop most of what used to be Forbes Field, but remnants remain. An original Forbes Field home plate lies beneath a glass casing in the floor of Posvar Hall's lobby. It's not exactly in the actual spot that home plate lay, but if one could triangulate the location of Moses' burning bush to within 81 feet of its exact location, no one would quibble (except perhaps a few Old Testament sabermetricians).

The University let stand approximately 180 feet of the outfield wall, which still shows two distance markers painted upon it. The original flag pole, located in the field of play in deepest center also remains. These things not only remain, they beckon.

On October 13, 1985, the 25th anniversary of the Pirates' triumph over the Yankees and of Mazeroski's homer, and at exactly 1:05, the actual game time, the late Saul Finkelstein, a local resident, went to the wall and listened to a tape recording of the broadcast. He did this by himself for eight years at which point Finkelstein told local author Jim

O'Brien his story which O'Brien then publicized. Shortly thereafter, other people began to join Finkelstein. On the occasion of the 50th anniversary in 2010, when a plaque commemorating Mazeroski's home run was dedicated, a thousand people attended, including the homer-hitting hero himself, as well as ten teammates.[58] As October 13th is a Holy Day in Pittsburgh, there is no place to be other than at the remnants of the Forbes Field Temple.

In Detroit, the Navin Field Grounds Crew has taken this reverence for the site of an old ballpark even further. Tiger Stadium once stood on the corner of Michigan and Trumbull Avenues, ground so familiar to Detroit fans that the spot is often simply referred to as "the Corner." Originally known as Navin Field and then Briggs Stadium, the park was abandoned by the Tigers in 1999 for their new Comerica Park. Ten years later it was torn down, but the diamond itself remained in the configuration that it always had since 1912. One day in 2010, and moved by the death of Ernie Harwell, the Tigers' Hall of Fame broadcaster, a 50 year old postal worker named Tom Derry stopped by the now empty lot to reminisce. The sacred ground was covered in weeds and garbage. He figured, "I got a riding mower, so I know I can cut the grass and I figured maybe some of my friends would want to volunteer, too."[59]

Friends did volunteer and soon the Navin Field Grounds Crew was born. They removed hundreds of pounds of trash. They brush-hogged multiple times. They were occasionally chased off by police because actually, they were trespassing on city property. They kept at it. They restored it, and people came and still do. They come to play baseball, they come to get married—Derry and his wife Sarah were married there in August, 2014—and they come to scatter the ashes of loved ones.[60] Perhaps most of all, they come to stand in the spot where their heroes once stood.

The Navin Field Grounds Crew has been the subject of an award-winning documentary entitled, *Stealing Home* and was featured in a *Rolling Stone* article. The City of Detroit finally came up with a plan to redevelop the site as the headquarters for the Police Athletic League. This would include a diamond, but according to the plans, it will be constructed with synthetic turf. This prompted an outcry from the Crew and others who cite the safety of the fill used in such construction among other items. Their real argument, however, is synthetic turf would destroy the sanctity of the site. Dirt and grass—always the grass!—is the portal to one's memories even if the grass growing there now isn't actually the same grass upon which Ty Cobb stood.[61] Cobb certainly never stood on synthetic grass in any case.

Despite the fact that Detroit's PAL has now taken over the site, the Navin Fields Ground Crew carries on and there is talk of adopting Hamtramck Stadium, one of 12 remaining Negro League ballparks. One can follow the activities of the Navin Field Grounds Crew through their Facebook page and their blog.[62] On my first visit to the page in October of 2014, I saw a photo of a couple with their dog, Ernie, who quite naturally was named for Ernie Harwell. The lady in the photo wrote in the comment section: "The sun was shining, I got to walk through Mickey Stanley territory, trace the base paths the Tigers ran, and stand at home where my ultimate favorite Bill Freehan caught. Life is good." A friend added, "Man, the grass looks beautiful."

As the effort of the Navin Field Grounds Crew demonstrates, ballparks are sanctified by virtue of who played there and by the generations who watched there. We separate this sacred space within the ballpark from the profane space without by clear lines of demarcation. The entrance to the new Comerica Park features a huge snarling tiger sitting in front of an iron header on which appears the name of the place. On top of each of the two brick structures that sit on either side of the gate, prowl two additional, snarling tigers. The heads of four more tigers decorate two sides each of the brick structures, casting a wary eye on all who pass below. Two giant baseball bats rise up at angles from the ground to a point above the brick wings. There is no doubt that once you pass over this threshold that you have passed from the streets of Detroit to the Land of the Tigers and it's possible that Tiger management placed all this over-sized Tiger bric-a-brack at the entrance in order to create an immediate sanctity. To paraphrase Lincoln at Gettysburg, however, ground cannot be consecrated on demand.

In his monograph, *The Sacred Spaces of Westminster*, one of my college professors, the late Dr. Ira Zepp, wrote that when we enter sacred space, "We are moving from disorder and the familiar to the ordered and unfamiliar."[63] Dr. Zepp didn't intend it, but that last sentence is the perfect description of attending a baseball game. Our lives are disordered, but familiar; baseball is oh, so orderly, but every game unfolds in a truly random, this-sequence-has-never-happened-before-and-never-will-again manner.

We consciously recognize and preserve and celebrate and defend the sacred space, but we are also responding on a much deeper level to the baseball diamond itself. Yes, the diamond is a square, but it functions as a circle, a characteristic which we recognize when we say "circle the bases." The circle is one of the oldest—and most sacred—symbols in human history. As Black Elk, an Oglala Sioux medicine man explained, "Everything tries to be round." American Indians have long celebrated the symbolism of the circle through the Hoop Dance. Tibetan Buddhists interpret Life through the intricate Bhavacakra or Wheel of Life. Then, there's the pitcher's mound, that circle from which the game proceeds, pitch by pitch, determining the opposition's travel around those touchstones we call bases. The batter starts at *home*, attempts to travel safely, and hopes to finish at *home* (and not *fourth base*). Zepp points out that the number *four* is sacred to many Indian tribes "precisely because of its all-embracing nature,"[64] an example of which would be the four points of the compass.

We think of the circle as a spatial concept, but mythologist Joseph Campbell notes that it has a spiritual aspect as well. "The temporal aspect of the circle is that you leave, go somewhere, and always come back. God is the alpha and the omega, the source and the end. The circle suggests immediately a completed totality, whether in time or in space."[65] From the first pitch until the last, the ball always emanates from that inner circle then returns to that inner circle that is the mound. The "totality" of the most linear of baseball's outcomes, the strikeout, is reinforced by the ritual, performed after the recording of every out when no one is on base, of throwing the ball around the infield rather than straight back to the pitcher. It is interesting to note that in all the discussion concerning speeding up the game, the removal of this ritual is never considered.

The mandala is an important symbol in Hinduism and Buddhism, but its description may sound familiar: "The basic form of most mandalas is a square with four gates containing a circle with a center point."[66] Campbell notes that a mandala is "a circle that is coordinated or symbolically designed so that it has the meaning of a cosmic order."[67] Perhaps, we never consider removing the ritual of throwing the ball around the infield because it would disrupt this cosmic order.

The distance between the "four gates" in baseball's mandala is, of course, 90'. Probably since 1857, when the 90' distance was officially established, baseball people have marveled at how 89' would be too short and 91' would be too long. It is a distance which requires flawless fielding and throwing to put out an average runner. It is a distance at which all-out hustle on every ground ball may produce a few extra infield hits in the course of the season and as we all know from the movie *Bull Durham*, the difference between a .250 hitter and a .300 hitter is just one of those extra infield hits per week. The 90' base line is one of humanity's most inspired creations.

The writer Thomas Wolfe made famous the phrase, "You can't go home again." This seems to be true everywhere but in the ballpark where the very object of the game is to go home again. Perhaps that's why Wolfe was such an ardent baseball fan. Surely, he would recognize that when Pirate fans gather at the wall or Detroit fans gather at The Corner, they are home. Al and I traveled from our respective homes in Florida and Maryland only to be home in Indiana. I'm at home when I talk to Mo. Is any place truly more sacred than home?

Cross the threshold of the nearest ballpark, whether it is constructed of steel and concrete or is more figurative such as the one that may exist on the airwaves of a phone call, and therein is a fellowship of believers, a circle unbroken. The world may be a Tower of Babel, but inside the ballpark everyone speaks the same language.

5 RELICS

The Baseball Hall of Fame in Cooperstown, New York, is not really a sacred space. It is a mecca to be sure and when pilgrims enter the actual hallowed Hall, they are reverent. The players whose bronze visages line the walls, however, did not do anything on that particular site to consecrate it. Rather, the Hall of Fame is a repository of their records and their relics of which there are so many, that one could spend days there without seeing them all. There are relics of the gods certainly—Babe Ruth and Honus Wagner and Ty Cobb and Bob Feller and Roberto Clemente and Mike Schmidt and Nolan Ryan—and there are relics of mere mortals who for one afternoon ascended Mt. Olympus. One can find at the Hall of Fame, for example, the ball from Bo Belinsky's no-hitter.[68]

Like the peasants of the middle ages, baseball people love relics. The on-line authority for the Catholic Church notes that there are three classes of relics: a body part from a saint, something worn or used by a saint, or "an object that has been touched to a first-class relic," i.e. one of the body parts.[69] I'm not sure that I quite understand this last one, but I liken it to cherishing the pen that Dave Boswell might have used to sign a 1969 Minnesota Twins playoff program. It's not the autograph itself, but it's something. A Class 2 baseball relic is simply defined as "game worn" or "game used." Insert either of those terms in front of an item and relic hunters begin to salivate to the point where Curt Schilling's bloody sock fetches a year's salary at auction.

Schilling pitched Game 6 of the 2004 American League

Championship Series for the Boston Red Sox against the hated New York Yankees. Down three games to none, the Red Sox won the next two, and now Schilling returned to the mound (after being defeated in Game One, giving up six runs in only three innings) even though the tendon in his ankle had been sutured into place because of an injury. The sutures separated, but Schilling pitched seven innings and only surrendered four hits, the television cameras zooming in on the bloody sock seemingly on every other pitch. Schilling won the game and the next day, Boston completed the comeback and defeated the Yankees.

The Red Sox went on to sweep the St. Louis Cardinals in the World Series, ending the Curse of the Bambino and bringing Boston its first World Championship in 86 years. Schilling pitched in the Series going six innings and giving up again, only one run on four hits, and bleeding all over his sock again. If you took that script to Hollywood most producers there would tell you that it was less realistic than *Field of Dreams*.

Schilling's bloodied white sanitary is as iconic in New England as Plymouth Rock. It is a relic, made sacred because it is a symbol of the possible in a world of the improbable. Such relics are priceless figuratively speaking anyway. The World Series sock fetched $92,613 in a 2013 auction of sports memorabilia when Schilling was forced to retrieve it from the Hall of Fame and sell it in order to pay off creditors from a business gone bad. As for the first sock, the one bloodied during the playoffs, Schilling threw it out after the game. We're not always aware of the sacred when it is encountered.

Fortunately, for most baseball players, fans have not (yet) demanded any first-class relics, and so what befell St. Thomas Aquinas has not befallen Babe Ruth. The former's mortal remains were "boiled by his confreres, so that they could sever, by one industrial act, the perishable flesh from the negotiable bones."[70] Babe Ruth has not been disinterred, but if I'm Mike Trout, I might want to keep my future burial site a secret.

Indeed, during the middle ages, trading in relics became a big business, which led to the widespread consecration of unauthenticated artifacts; so much so, that after visiting Europe and the Holy Land, Mark Twain wrote, "We find a piece of the true cross in every old church we go into, and some of the nails that held it together. I would not like to be positive, but I think we have seen as much of a keg of these nails."[71]

Baseball people will recognize a similar pattern in modern relic collecting: the demand for such items is so great that "relics" are being produced by the keg-full and are, thereby, reduced to the mere level of "souvenir." Separating the relic from the souvenir has led to an entire industry of graders and authenticators for autographs, equipment, and cards. One wonders if the Bloody Sock came with the results of a DNA test.

Not even the Hall of Fame's collection can compare, however, to the sacred items to be found in attics, basements, and bedrooms. Sure, Cooperstown's collection of artifacts is sacred because of its historic nature, but of far greater sanctity are those relics which we have personally gathered from the gods or from the important baseball events in our own histories.

Or a relic that simply says, "I was there," which is the beauty of the baseball scorecard that says not only, "I was there," but "I participated" as well. You can use the simple one that appears in the middle of most programs or design your own or copy a free one from the Internet or purchase Bob Carpenter's Official Fan Scorebook that contains room for 100 games for only $30.00 plus $5.00 shipping and handling. Bob Carpenter is the television voice of the Washington Nationals and his scorebook is very impressive although I have designed my own. (Of course.) I record the weather, the start time and end time, unusual plays, when the moon came up, funny remarks from fans, and any other occurrence that helps me re-create the experience. College and minor league scorecards are always fun to look at say, ten years after the fact and discover for example, that in that 17 inning game played in Luray that the Wranglers' second baseman, Daniel Murphy, became the Mets' and now the Nationals' second baseman Daniel Murphy.

Becky, has an unusual relic, one that definitely says, "I was there." There's a little scar on her ankle where Oriole minor-leaguer Hayden Penn accidentally stepped on her with his cleat while he was playing for Delmarva and she was working as an on-field promo girl for the Hagerstown Suns. We hoped that Penn would make it big and then she could really get the conversation started at any party by taking off her shoe. Alas, Penn, who was a big-time prospect, fizzled accumulating a 4-6 record in 33 big league games for three different teams. Now that little scar is a conversation starter only among those who speak baseball.

More normal relics include official programs, yearbooks, ticket stubs, and pennants. David B. Stinson still has the program from that Oriole game that he attended with his dad for his birthday, a program made even more sacred by the fact that, after the game, Paul Blair, the Birds' eight-time Gold Glove center-fielder, autographed it. We don't need a certificate of authenticity for our experiences, although proof that they really happened is valuable. I have reached an age where I may momentarily wonder if an episode from my past really happened or if I'm actually remembering an episode of some old TV show. Baseball relics not only reinforce the memory of "I was there!" they confirm the sense of "I was, then!"

A captured foul ball not only says, "I was there," it also says, "I participated!" even more so than keeping score. The mad scramble for a foul ball often resembles a mini-riot. YouTube is full of foul ball videos; of people diving, jumping, and injuring themselves trying to retrieve the relic that tells the story of how, "Hunter Pence fouled off a 2-1 pitch from Dan Haren in San Francisco last year *and I caught it!*"

Only twice in the 52 years that I have been attending professional baseball games have I had an encounter with a foul ball. Some twelve years ago, while sitting in the top row of the third base bleachers at Municipal Stadium in Hagerstown, a foul ball was lofted in my direction. I stretched my bare hand over the rail and it hit right in my palm. There was too much spin on the ball, however, and it twisted out of my hand before I could even close my fingers. It fell to the concourse below where some little kid scrambled after it. A couple of years later, at a poorly attended Carolina League playoff game, I was leisurely spread out across several seats along the first base side when Oriole prospect Nolan Reimold swung late and whistled one towards my largely empty section. The ball arrived in my vicinity much faster than I had anticipated and clattered around under the empty seats very near me.

Fortunately, I arrived at it before most of the little kids had even risen from their seats and I had my first foul ball. I had the proper sense of baseball decorum not to hold it aloft with the expectation that others would applaud my feat. Holding a ball on high after merely picking it up rather than catching it is akin to bringing a ball from home and holding it up. The energy exerted is about the same.

As a result of that experience, I gained two valuable things. First, of course, I have the ball which I inscribed right below the scuff mark, *Nolan Reimold foul ball during K in 8th in. Keys v Kinston Game #3 Finals 9/11/06 Keys lose 2-1in 11 in. 1st foul ball I ever got!* Second, I have the knowledge that I should no longer try to catch foul balls because my reflexes are clearly nowhere near what they used to be.

Baseball cards, at least for people my age are most definitely a cardboard passport to yesterday. I still have my first two (of course) cut from the back of Jell-O boxes in 1962: Jim Gentile and Ron Hansen, early Oriole heroes. I collected almost the entire 1966 Topps set, one five-card pack at a time, but was missing two cards from the second series and many from the always difficult seventh series. I completed the set when I was in my forties, but I'm fairly certain that I could go through those cards right now and tell you which ones showed up underneath that pink wad of gum and which were purchased years later at card shows, because the former whisk me back to those Saturdays when I took my $.25 weekly allowance to Sewell's General Store and bought five packs of Topps baseball cards. They confirm that I was, then. The cards I bought later are the mere completion of a childhood mission.

Everyone knows someone whose mom threw out their card collection, and there are plenty of stories about kids inadvertently playing with priceless autographed balls; the plot of *The Sandlot* revolves around boys trying to retrieve a baseball autographed by Babe Ruth that one of them hit into the neighbor's yard which is guarded by a mastiff.

Occasionally, someone willfully dispossesses a relic (as opposed to a souvenir), usually while under the influence of love. A friend of mine, Lynne Marino told me a story that will produce a reflexive cringe in any baseball person:

When my mom (who was born in 1927) was a kid in St. Louis, you could take the streetcar to the old Sportsman's Park. She would often go (without her parents) with different kids from the neighborhood to the games and sit in the bleacher seats, taking her baseball glove with her. She was there when Stan the Man hit a grand slam right into the bleachers, and she caught the ball. Stan signed it, and she promptly gave it to a boy she had a crush on.

Stan hit nine grand slams in his career and it's likely that Lynne's mom, Ruth Jungmann, witnessed his first one on September 22, 1942 off Pittsburgh's Rip Sewell in the bottom of the 5th inning. This seems likely as Musial's next grand slam in St. Louis was not until July of 1948, when Ruth was 21, two years out of high school, and probably past taking her glove to the park.

Apoplectic would be a good description of Lynne's reaction when she first heard this story from her mom. I'm almost afraid to tell her that this could have been Stan the Man's first grand slam which would make the autographed ball a most-coveted relic indeed. I am sure, however, that Ruth's story is not unique. I imagine that many a home run and foul ball has been presented as a token of love.

Increasingly, the television cameras record an adult scrambling for a ball who then turns around and gives it to a youngster. I think most young men make this gesture in order to impress young women. I am now above impressing women, young or old, and so if I am seated close to you and a batted ball comes flying in our direction, I am offering no quarter and expect none in return; if it lands near where I'm ducking, it's mine and I'm not giving it to any little kid, either. It's not my fault that their reach isn't as long as mine.

Then there is the relic, not from a game or a player, but from one's personal past. Baseball people may buy new baseball gloves, but they never get rid of their old ones. The Wilson, Dual-Hinged Ron Santo Model that I used in high school to play third base was used by Becky when she was in middle school to play third base. The cloth tab on the strap is gone and the leather is now weak. It has been used up to its last, which means that its value has increased; not as a glove itself, of course, but as a relic.

I still have the first baseball glove that I ever owned, the one with which I first played catch. I had Brooks Robinson autograph it when he was the featured attraction at the 1965 Carrol Manor Recreation Baseball Opening Day Ceremonies. It's faded badly, but if I pointed out the signature to you, you'd be able to see it. When I asked Martha to marry me, I gave her two items: a ring, of course, because this is engagement protocol, and the glove. The former showed that I was serious; the second showed that our love was forever in both directions, for Martha was getting not only all of my tomorrows, but all of my yesterdays as well.

Bats are a different story, mainly because they break. I am no expert on wood composition, but I have developed a theory that the amount of time it takes for a bat to break is inversely proportional to the amount of money spent on it. Because a bat rarely survives childhood, a bat is more of an icon than a relic, but a powerful one nonetheless. Put a bat in the hands of anyone who played baseball and he or she will immediately check its balance, its heft, and its grain in order to pronounce it a good bat or not. As a sign of my age, when I refer to baseball bats, I am of course, referring to *wooden* baseball bats. Those aluminum concoctions that look like something out of *Star Wars* and cost something along the lines of *Star Wars'* budget are not true baseball bats. After all, if Bernard Malamud had played with an aluminum bat when he was a kid, he could have never written *The Natural*.

If each baseball person is his own priest, then each baseball person determines the sanctity of the items that he or she possesses. I don't "own" Dick Hall's autograph—that was bestowed upon me when I was seven or eight while on a shopping trip to Montgomery Wards in downtown Baltimore where my parents and I spied the Oriole relief pitcher and his wife. My mom spoke to him, and finding a scrap of paper in her purse, asked him for an autograph for me, which he smilingly obliged. I can see the entire scene yet. At some point, this relic will revert back to a simple scrap of paper with the name of a forgotten ballplayer written across it, but that's okay. My grandchildren will need their own set of saints. A collector may assign a value to my Dick Hall autograph and seeing as how it is not on a card or a ball or a program or a game worn jersey, I can imagine that it isn't very high. Collectors always take into account condition, but often they don't know how to value yesterdays.

Baseball relics transport us to a decade, a season, or a game from our past. We are in two moments at the same time and thus, at least momentarily we taste immortality ourselves. We will never have a line in *Baseball Encyclopedia* but the moment that the relic represents is recorded in our *Personal Encyclopedia* where it remains for all time, or at least for all our time.

6 HOLY GHOSTS

The New York Yankees began a tradition in 1932, when the team erected the first monument in what would be known as Monument Park in honor of former manager Miller Huggins who had died before the end of the 1929 season. Lou Gehrig was the first to have his number retired on that memorable Independence Day in 1939—a game which my friend Mo Weber attended—and teams have been erecting statues and monuments, and retiring numbers ever since.

Teams in other sports erect statues and retire numbers as well, but the unique nature of baseball, wherein players consistently occupy a certain portion of the field because it is their *position*, means that particular spaces within the larger confines of the ballpark themselves become sacred. Hence, visitors to the site of old Tiger Stadium in Detroit can "walk through Mickey Stanley territory." Even if the grass isn't the same, it is the same intrinsic space.

Unlike other sports where the players are all over the gridiron, court, rink, or pitch, baseball players begin each play in a single spot, almost becoming living statues themselves in the moment before the ball is delivered. A Cubs fan can look down at third base in Wrigley Field and still *see* Ron Santo crouching there. A Dodger fan can look out at the mound in Dodger Stadium and still *see* Sandy Koufax bent over staring in for the sign, his arms dangling at his sides. A fan can glance at the left-hand batter's box in Fenway Park, and still *see* Ted Williams, his hands just below the letters, the bat almost perpendicular to the ground. No baseball person is really surprised to see Shoeless Joe Jackson step out of the corn and onto a baseball diamond in the middle of Iowa. For baseball people, this is a common experience at any ballpark. We no longer see through a glass darkly upon entering these temples known as ballparks for they light the way of memory and allow us to see face to face, whether that face is Ted Williams or Ted Lepcio.[72]

I have already referenced Municipal Stadium in Hagerstown, Maryland, the closest professional ballpark to where we used to live, just eight miles up the road from our house. It is the home of the Suns who completed their 36th season in 2016. Municipal Stadium, was erected in 1930 for the Hagerstown Hubs of the Blue Ridge League. The Hubs moved to Parkersburg, West Virginia during the 1931 season and a host of professional teams played at Municipal Stadium sporadically until 1981 when the Suns began their current run. Since that time, a variety of features have been tacked on to the place and it's a hodge-podge of bleachers and concession stands. Many great ballplayers have played for Hagerstown from Matt Cain to Michael Young to Carlos Gomez to Bryce Harper, but when I gaze across the diamond I see Becky who, as I mentioned worked for the Suns as a promo girl from 2004-2005. She graduated from Williamsport High School (one year behind Nick Adenhart[73]) as the Class of 2005 valedictorian, and Martha and I felt that it would be appropriate if the Suns recognized her accomplishment by having her throw out the first pitch.

Martha called the Suns' management and they were more than happy to oblige. It was often Becky's duty to escort the ceremonial first pitcher to the mound and that June evening, Becky was handed two baseballs, but only one person to escort, much to her confusion. When the public address announcer let it be known that there was a second ceremonial first pitch, she grew worried that she had missed bringing someone onto the field. As soon as the word *valedictorian* echoed around Municipal Stadium, however, she knew what was afoot. To me, she remains forever on that mound, in that wonderful summer that separates high school from college, a broad smile on her face and her whole life before her.

It's not just the players who consecrate ballparks.

Byron Bennett, the hero of David B. Stinson's *Deadball*, also played in Hagerstown, and it was at Municipal Stadium that I met this fellow writer and fan. In 2012, David took me on a tour of Baltimore's lost ballparks. Using photographs and written descriptions, he was sure that he had located the exact layout of Union Park and so, we parked the car and made our way down an alley. David pointed to the basement door of a row house about 60 feet from where we stood.

"We're standing on the spot of the pitcher's mound," he said excitedly, "and just behind that door was home plate." David was so in the moment that I looked to my right, half-expecting to see John McGraw and Hughie Jennings manning the left side of the Oriole infield.

The final stop on the tour that day was the site of Memorial Stadium, a stop that I wasn't sure I wanted to make. Al and I had driven past a couple of years before and that day, as we turned down 33rd Street, I had that same excited feeling that I used to get when the ballpark first came into view. I can't say that I expected to see it, but I was overwhelmed with disappointment when it wasn't there. Al clearly felt the same and we drove past as fast as we could, but now David wanted to actually stop and visit. I discovered, however, that the Cal Ripken, Sr. Foundation had erected a kid-sized ballpark on the site, and home plate still looked out on those white houses that stood beyond the scoreboards which framed center field. A plaque commemorating the great Oriole and Colt football teams that played on this ground stood outside the backstop. I almost felt dizzy when we first pulled into the parking lot, the kind of dizzy one might feel when returning home after burying a loved one only to find her reading glasses on top of a book that was marked half-way through. Now, however, seeing this little field whose little batters would look out on the same backdrop restored a certain sense of balance.

At some point in life, somewhere in the neighborhood of 50, time begins to warp. There is a certain inner chaos that exists because by now we have been many ages which we may have outgrown, but have never abandoned. Most people conceive of Life as being linear, but baseball reminds us to live within the circle. If we do, we come back around to the nine-year old within who remembers a certain wisdom that our contemporary selves have forgotten. Looking out at the white houses, but not seeing the ballpark that framed them had made me feel as empty as the space itself until a little voice noted how cool it would be to play on the same field that Brooks Robinson played on. That thought filled the empty space and I came away happy that David had insisted on the visit. Or, as Black Elk said, "The life of a man is a circle from childhood to childhood, and so it is in everything where power moves."[74] It doesn't even matter that most of the nine-year olds who play there have no idea who Brooks Robinson was and the only football team they know is the Baltimore Ravens. It made *my* inner nine-year old feel better.

I came away happy and with two souvenirs. When Memorial Stadium was torn down, the rubble was simply bulldozed smooth and most of it was buried beneath the parking lot that services the little field and the YMCA that was also built on the site. More than a decade has passed now and bits of brick and concrete are making their way to the surface of the grassy medians and the areas outside the miniature diamond. I picked up most of a brick and a bit of concrete. I believe, I mean *I believe* that the brick came from the players' entrance and witnessed everyone who ever wore an Oriole uniform through 1991. I believe that the chunk of concrete was from the dugout steps. I can't prove that, of course, but you gotta believe. I put these relics in a cabinet right next to my vile of Memorial Stadium infield dirt. There is no doubt that the dirt came from Memorial Stadium's infield because the certificate of authenticity is signed by not only Mr. Jim Palmer, but also by Mr. Brooks Robinson. That makes it as certain as the sunrise.

Three items were, in fact, officially removed from Memorial Stadium and transferred to Oriole Park at Camden Yards when the former was closed. One was home plate which was ceremoniously dug up after the final game and driven by limo to what was then the new park, where it was ceremoniously dropped into place. (Except it wasn't. A replica plate was used because Camden Yards wasn't quite ready for a home plate to be installed, and the replica is what the crowd saw on the scoreboard back at Memorial Stadium during the closing ceremonies.)

Second, the right field foul pole was removed and then erected later at Camden Yards. A little bronze plaque right below the pole informs folks that they are beholding a relic. Third, and most poignantly, some lettering from Memorial's façade was also moved to a spot just outside Camden Yards' entrance. The old ballpark had undergone a name change from "Municipal Stadium" to "Memorial Stadium" in 1950 to honor those who had served in World War II. The entire dedication, written in large aluminum letters, appeared on the front of the stadium, but it was the letters of the last sentence that were removed to Camden: *Time Will Not Dim The Glory of Their Deeds.* Memorial Stadium was a sacred space on multiple levels.

Of course, I remember the last game played at Memorial Stadium. Actually, that's not quite accurate. I don't remember much about the game except that the Orioles absorbed yet another loss in that 1991 season, 7-1 to the Tigers. I remember that, and the fact that Mike Flanagan, now at the end of his career and one of the last active links to the glory years of 1979-1983, was brought on to record the final two outs, which he did, both by strike out.

None of the 50,700 in attendance cared that the Orioles lost. They in the park and thousands of us at home in front of the television were waiting for that final good-bye. Rumor was that numerous former players would return for the commemoration. The field was cleared and silence pervaded the old ballpark. Then the theme from *Field of Dreams*—what else?—began to play and I'm guessing that after three notes 25,350 people were in tears. The first player to emerge from the dugout, Brooks Robinson—who else?—in uniform jogged with his glove to third base and as was his habit, smoothed the dirt with his cleat. Now, everyone in the stadium was in tears, we were in tears at home and as the players kept coming—Frank and Boog; Palmer and Dempsey; Flanagan, McGregor, Tippy; Elrod, Belanger, and Luis Aparicio; Jim Gentile, the tears kept flowing. I'm crying now as I write this.

In all, 78 players emerged from the dugout and waved to the fans.[75] I know that because I pulled my file for that season and found that number. There was the front page of *The Sun* that featured a photo that I remember so well. In it, a fan identified as Greg Lockwood is standing with his arms raised, a well-worn glove in one hand, his Oriole hat in the other, tears streaming down his face. There was a smaller photo there to the left of the copy that I had not remembered. It was of Mike Flanagan, the sleeve of his jacket covering his left arm, his Oriole hat raised on high as a thank you for the curtain call he received for closing out Memorial Stadium in two-strikeout style. He looks sad, grim even. Clearly, this good-bye was painful for him. It's a haunting photo to look back upon. Flanagan, one of the wittiest Orioles to ever don the uniform would become the team's executive vice-president of baseball operations in 2006, and failing in his efforts to restore his team to glory, would kill himself on August 24, 2011, just a few months before the Orioles' renaissance.

Say it ain't so.

Yes, kid, I'm afraid it is.

We may shed tears for those diamond ghosts who have been uprooted from their grassy haunts, but truly we weep for the ghosts in the stands who have lost a home when the bleachers come down: the ghosts of our dads and moms and friends; and the ghosts of our own children when they still held our hands and asked permission to walk down by the dugout. Ghosts of former selves. The little boy that I was, sitting in the upper deck on a sunny Saturday in early October *knowing* that Paul Blair could hit a home run and knowing nothing of aging or death or of disappointment beyond getting triples of a Roger Repoz baseball card instead of the Dave Johnson that I needed. The world seemed complete, without beginning or end and nowhere was that more true for me than at Memorial Stadium.

The actual attendance that day was well beyond 50,700 if you count the ghosts.

***

Often, we forget that the ghosts on the field were actual people who were absorbing their own experiences. In 1999, Moe Drabowsky, the former Oriole reliever who still holds the World Series record of 11 strikeouts by a relief pitcher which occurred in Game One of the 1966 World Series, was the pitching coach of the Delmarva Shorebirds, a Class A affiliate of Baltimore's in the South Atlantic League. That's the league that the Suns are in, and one summer night I ran down to the rail in Hagerstown after the game to give Moe a shout, a "thank you" as it were for the memories. I wanted to let him know that *he* meant something to me, not just the 11 Dodger whiffs.

"Moe! Everyone remembers the World Series," I yelled as he ambled toward the clubhouse, "but I remember that you had to make an emergency start that year and—"

"I beat Pete Richert down in Washington that night, 2-1. I went 8 2/3 innings!" he said, completing my sentence. We chatted a bit more and then he continued his walk down the right field warning track to the clubhouse. Becky, still has the ball that we asked Moe to sign. Clearly, I had reached into Moe's *Personal Encyclopedia* and now, whenever I hear the name *Moe Drabowsky*, my immediate image is of a man whose eyes lit up and whose joy was as fresh as if it were August of 1966 and we were talking in Washington after that game. He was a childhood hero, standing there on the Municipal Stadium warning track in his uniform, a God descended from Mt. Olympus, but for the moment, we were just two guys talking about a baseball game. We were speaking the same language.

Moe Drabowsky gave Becky and me something far more precious than the autographed ball. He shared *his* memory; he shared his humanity. Since that moment, Moe is for me, not only a childhood hero, but an adulthood hero as well.

The Hero: He is perhaps the most significant and recognizable archetype in human experience and it's been said that our admiration of modern athletes, an admiration bordering on worship, is a fulfillment of this ancient archetype. The traditional hero is either a warrior who conquers some monster—be it Beowulf slaying Grendel or George Washington defeating the monstrous oppression of the British—or one who embarks upon a spiritual quest and returns to the rest of us with insight into our human condition; think religious figures such as Buddha or Jesus; or poets or artists or novelists such as James Joyce. Or W. P. Kinsella.

The traditional hero usually has a set of trials he must endure to prove himself worthy. Hercules had 12 labors to perform for example, that prepared him to be the hero that he became. In baseball, these "trials" are called "the minor leagues" and they hold a special attraction for baseball people. With few exceptions, the best amateur players, once they are signed to play professional baseball are now among the worst professional players and they must start their careers in places such as Bluefield, Wheeling, and Missoula. After three to five years, they have been tempered by endless bus rides and thousands of ground balls at 2:00 in the afternoon in empty stadiums. Should they reach the major leagues, they are called "rookies."

Howard Sensel described the heroism that is particular to the minor leagues and why he found it so attractive:

In the minor leagues, the game was played mostly by grown men who would never be famous and who would never be rich, men who would always travel by rented school bus and always stay in fleabag hotels. These were grown men playing baseball who had to sacrifice money and comfort in order to play. And that is a kind of heroism that is larger and more noble than any superhuman athletic dexterity.[76]

This is the appeal of the character of Crash Davis in the movie *Bull Durham*, a character made all the more compelling because there are dozens of Crash Davis' all over the minor leagues. Take Marshall Brant, for example, about whom Dick Schaap wrote a piece five years before *Bull Durham* was released. In August of 1983, when the article appeared in *Parade Magazine*, Brant had been in the minors for nine seasons. He received $14.00 per day meal money when the major league equivalent was $41.50. He had reached the majors in 1980, appearing in three games for the New York Yankees (after the Yankees had won the division) coming to bat six times, striking out three, and never reaching base. He remained in the Yankees minor league system, playing at Triple A Columbus and putting up stellar numbers. In 1982, he was named an International League and AAA all-star, but no major league teams expressed any interest in the 6'5", 185 pound first baseman. In 1983, the Yankees sent "a fine young prospect" named Don Mattingly to Columbus to sharpen his hitting skills. On June 15 of that season, Brant was traded to the Oakland A's along with Ben Callahan for pitcher Matt Keough. Assigned to Oakland's Triple A Tacoma squad, Brant was called up to the big club just a few days later where he collected his first major league hit, RBI, and run scored.

"Brant may not finish the season in the big leagues, may never spend a full year in the big leagues. But he has a hit, he has an RBI, and he has memories that most minor leaguers, most professional baseball players, will never have," wrote Schaap.[77]

Marshall Brant would collect one more hit, RBI, and run in 14 more plate appearances before being sent down to Tacoma in July. After the 1983 season, Brant retired from baseball. As of 2015, he was a salesman for McConnell Chevrolet in Healdsburg, California 90 minutes up U. S. 101 from his home in Santa Rosa.[78] The Goodwill Series Marshall Brant Tournament has been held since 2009 in Hillsburg, California.

Although his career major league average stands for all time at .100, Marshall Brant is a hero. Ask any Joe Boyd, the main character from the under-rated baseball play/movie *Damn Yankees* who sits on his front porch listening to a game and whispers into the night that he'd sell his soul for just one crack at becoming Joe Hardy.

Brant gave it his best, which ironically, is probably more than we can say for Babe Ruth. Ruth performed heroic feats arguably beyond those of any other baseball player in history. The Babe, however, was blessed with enormous natural talent and his biographers tell us that he wasn't exactly a paragon of clean living. Babe Ruth is a hero for his feats. Marshall Brant is a hero for his struggles.

Brant, however, at least reached the major leagues and enjoyed a Moonlight Graham moment. Most minor-leaguers, of course, will be released or sustain career-ending injuries long before they get close to the big time.

Take the case of Marc Heyison, who was drafted by the Orioles out of George Washington University in June of 1983, and featured in Marc Gunther's 1984 book, *Basepaths: From the Minors to the Big Leagues and Beyond*. Gunther's book examines baseball as a career and includes stories and interviews with Ferguson Jenkins, "Catfish" Hunter, Bill White and others, famous and not famous. *The Sun Magazine*, a supplement to Baltimore's *Sunday Sun*, excerpted the chapter on Heyison who spent the summer of 1983 playing Rookie League ball for the Bluefield Orioles in the Appalachian League.[79] Heyison hit .240 playing third base for Bluefield. Promoted to Hagerstown, then in the Class A Carolina League for 1984, he went 3-for-15 before a degenerative shoulder ended his career.

Playing shortstop next to Heyison in Bluefield was another first year player named Bill Ripken, whose brother Cal had played shortstop for Bluefield in 1978, and who would win the Most Valuable Player award for the World Champion Orioles in 1983. Bill, and pitcher Mark Leiter, were the only two players on Bluefield's roster to make the major leagues. The Pikeville Cubs also produced two future major leaguers while the Bristol Tigers and Elizabethton Twins produced three each. The Pulaski Braves produced one. The Paintsville Brewers' roster contained an unbelievable nine future big-leaguers including Glen Bragg, Chris Bosio, and Dan Plesac. No one on the Johnson City Cardinals reached The Show. Of the approximately 200 players who played in the Appalachian League that summer, 19, or about 10% ever got to the major leagues.

Such odds are exactly why many of us strongly identify with the players who spent a summer or two or ten climbing Mount Olympus, but never making it to the top, because anyone who ever played Little League spent at least one summer trying to ascend that mountain. We can't imagine what that view is like from the top, but we can imagine what it's like from just above where we made it.

You sit down at the desk of your car salesman and notice on the wall behind him a black and white photo of a guy sliding across home, his Columbus Clippers helmet flying off his head as he reaches for the dish with his hand, the on-deck batter waving him to the outside part of the plate. It's him, your car salesman, and you immediately ask, "What was it like?" And what you mean is "What was the view from your place on the mountain?"

Marc Heyison scaled other heights. The would-be major leaguer, whose first name was, ironically enough misspelled *Mark* by *The Sun Magazine*, is the CEO of Top Notch, Inc. a company specializing in promotional items as well as imprinted and embroidered clothing in College Park, Maryland. In 1999, he co-founded Men Against Breast

Cancer after his mother Gloria had been diagnosed with it several years earlier. He has been elected to George Washington University's Hall of Fame.

Minor league or major league, or in any sport for that matter, we immediately recognize the warrior hero, whether it's the batter who blasts a game-winning home run or the quarterback who outwits the cornerback and tosses a perfect touchdown pass. Physical conquest is frequently seen in sports, but upon reflection it is obvious that the athlete is also a spiritual hero as well, for he must be on a journey, one that takes him inward. He has to have mastered this journey or there would be no competing at the highest level. Joseph Campbell, who studied and taught comparative mythology for over 50 years, and wrote extensively about the hero, commented upon this: "The place to find is within yourself. I learned a little about this in athletics. The athlete who is in top form has a quiet place within himself, and it's around this, somehow, that his action occurs. If he's all out there in the action field, he will not be performing properly."[80]

Only in baseball do we continuously see athletes finding the "quiet place within." The pitcher must apply all he knows about the mechanics of his trade to place the ball precisely where he wants it, without giving it any thought. The batter must apply the same process as must the fielder. Each has a multitude of time to think about what he is doing which would be completely counterproductive to what he is trying to accomplish. Going to the quiet place is an imperative for success. Cal Ripken once explained it this way: "You're at the plate with 50,000 fans on their feet screaming, and it's totally quiet in your mind. When you hit the ball and start running, about halfway to first the sound comes back into your head. There's no better feeling."[81] Or as Yogi Berra said, "I can't think and hit at the same time."

The field goal, the penalty shot, the free throw offer such moments in other sports, but baseball is a continuous sequence of such moments and baseball people appreciate the rare quality that allows a human being to field a two-hop ground ball with a runner on third in the bottom of the 9th of the Seventh Game of the World Series with his team up by one run and 50,000 people willing him to make an error, and then throw it chest high to the first baseman as if it were the 5th inning of a meaningless exhibition game in March. If you have ever stood over a two foot putt and knew beyond a shadow of a doubt that, even if the hole were as big as a garbage can lid, you still couldn't make it, then you have a sense of how difficult it is to find the quiet place within on demand and regardless of the situation.

This inner journey takes place play after play, game after game, season after season and is the solution for what Campbell viewed as the problem in a modern society that changes so quickly "that there is no time for anything to constellate itself before it's thrown over again."[82] That statement sounds remarkably like Terrance Mann's speech in *Field of Dreams*, in which he tells Ray that, "The one constant through all the years, Ray, has been baseball. America has rolled by like an army of steamrollers. It has been erased like a blackboard, rebuilt and erased again. But baseball has marked the time."

Baseball has done more than "mark the time"; it has solved the problem of constancy in two ways. First, baseball very deliberately keeps the quest the same for the most part, which is why 40 years after its introduction the designated hitter rule continues to cause many heated discussions.[83] Rule changes have been abundant in other sports and indeed, the mere size and speed of modern football and basketball players has radically changed the way those games are played. Resurrect Cy Young and place him on a modern mound, however, and he's still going to attempt to hit the outside corner for strike one. (Although he might laugh himself silly at the terms "pitch count" and "innings limit.") Thus, to use Campbell's term, baseball through its consistency over the last century has "institutionalized" the hero's message: Go within to conquer that which is without.

Second, the baseball hero myth stays relevant because rather than changing the quest, baseball changes heroes. They remain relevant because each generation chooses its own. A simple review of one's baseball cards reveals that the heroes pictured represent the successive generations. Check out Steve Barber's crew cut on his 1962 Topps # 355 card or Bob Miller's bristly hair style on his 1963 Topps # 261 card. Turn ahead a dozen years and check out Jim Grant's muttonchops on Topps #

111 or all that hair sticking out of Pat Dobson's hat on Topps 1973 # 34. (Nothing compares, however, to Oscar Gamble's afro on his 74T Topps Traded Series card from 1976.) Think of all those mustaches of the 1970s "Swingin' A's" of Oakland. Or the beards and tattoos on today's players. Babe Ruth gives way to Lou Gehrig who gives way to Joe DiMaggio who gives way to Mickey Mantle. In a few more years there was Guidry and Jackson. A few years later, Pettitte and Jeter. As Paul Tillich wrote, "A god disappears; divinity remains." Baseball keeps us connected to the divine or at least to those moments of immortal sublimity. In this way, it also keeps us connected to each other. The son can only understand his father's reverence for Mickey Mantle through his own reverence for Derek Jeter. Otherwise, Mantle is just an Okie on a piece of cardboard, albeit with some gaudy statistics on the back.

We are connected directly to our baseball heroes even if the connection is not immediate. From the back yard to Little League to Pony League to high school, maybe to college, on to the professional ranks and through the minors, up to the majors and in the case of that 1978 Bluefield Oriole shortstop, to the Hall of Fame. We might have stopped at the first link in that chain, but we're still part of the chain.

I hit one home run during my high school career. When I think of that moment—the pitch was down and away and I swear I saw the bat connect with the ball which rose about four feet off the ground and sailed about one foot above the chain link right-center field fence—I can't imagine that any homer that Cal Ripken ever hit meant more to him than that one did to me. Maybe (probably) I just got lucky, but I found my quiet place within.

I found it again during one of Loch Raven High School's greatest baseball games ever played. Our ace, Bob Stagge, whose dad sat on the hill with my father and with Al's, took a perfect game into the bottom of the 7th (the final inning in high school games) against Milford Mill. We were winning 2-0; I had tripled and scored the second run. Bob got two outs in the 7th and I crouched at third base wanting the ball to be hit to me. *I knew* that if I got it, Bob would have his perfect game. A two-hopper was hit to my left. I gloved it and threw chest-high to first baseman Bernie Cavanaugh and Bob had his perfect game. I had seven total chances, a chance per inning, a hand in one-third of the outs Bob needed. I had reached a special place, indeed, a sacred place within myself. Yes, it was on some high school field that didn't even have dugouts, in a game that mattered to precious few people besides Mr. Stagge, Mr. Smith, and my dad. It was against a bunch of other kids, none of whom played professionally either, in front of perhaps 20 people. It may have only been one high school game as opposed to say 2,632 consecutive major league games, but for that one game, I played in the same internal place that Cal Ripken played. Cal and me, links on the chain.

7 MIRACLES

Baseball is full of miracles. The Miracle on Coogan's Bluff. The Miracle Mets. The Miracle Braves. That last mentioned miracle took place all the way back in 1914 when the Boston Braves, who found themselves in last place on the Fourth of July, stormed to the National League pennant, winning by 10.5 games over the second place New York Giants and sweeping the favored Philadelphia Athletics in the World Series. Some people view this as baseball's biggest miracle still, if not its most recent.[84]

Then, of course, there are the heal-the-sick type of miracles, the most famous occurring in October of 1926 when Babe Ruth promised a home run for 11-year old Johnny Sylvester who was suffering from osteomyelitis, the result of falling from a horse. Hearing of Sylvester's plight, both World Series teams, the Yankees and Cardinals sent autographed balls to the hospital. Ruth added to his autograph, "I'll knock a homer for you in Wednesday's game." He did. In fact, the Babe hit three homers in that Game 4, although the Cardinals won in seven games when for some inexplicable reason, Ruth decided to steal second with New York down by a run and two out in the bottom of the 9th. The Babe proved to be a better miracle worker than a base stealer as he was thrown out, but Johnny Sylvester got well, eventually attended Princeton, became a submarine commander during World War II, and later a president of Amscomatic Corporation.[85]

Ruth's exploits have become so legendary that some have doubted the veracity of this story, but a 2008 article in the *New York Daily News* not only verifies the details, but was written to note that a plaque commemorating the event was to be placed on the site of Sylvester's former home in Essex Fells, New Jersey.[86] Johnny's son and Ruth's daughter were on hand for the commemoration of which exists a YouTube video.

If you had to pick one baseball player in the whole history of the game to hit a home run on demand, it would be Babe Ruth. . . . Osteomyelitis is not fatal. . . . Players making kind gestures to sick kids is not unusual, *but still* . . . A home run is an improbable outcome on *any* at-bat. Ruth is second on the all-time at-bats per home runs list at 11.76 (Mark McGwire's 10.61 is the top mark) which means that the Babe hit a homer less than 10% of the time that he came to the plate.

The real miracle here to me is that it never seemed to cross the Babe's mind that he might disappoint a sickly kid. *That* is finding the quiet place within, although by all accounts, that was the only quiet place in which The Babe ever spent any time.

Bob Aspromonte, of the Houston Colt .45s, now Astros, on the other hand, had the good sense to promise a blind kid who asked for a special homer that "If I do hit one tonight, it will be for you." Aspromonte, however, had a career at-bats per home run rate of 79.89 and a total of eleven home runs in his then two-year old career coming into the game against the Giants at Houston on July 25, 1962. He was in a slump to boot. No doubt nine-year old Bill Bradley, who had been rendered blind by a lightning strike in May, had not been taught probability. Aspromonte, Billy's favorite player, went to Houston Methodist Hospital where Billy was receiving treatment during the day of the 25th, bearing the obligatory autographed baseball, which is apparently a token of an impending miracle.[87]

On a 2-1 pitch from Stu Miller in the bottom of the 8th, with the bases empty, Aspromonte hit one out. Everyone in the park knew about the third baseman's visit to the blind boy and as the ball sailed out of Colt Stadium, Houston announcer Gene Elston exuberantly proclaimed "This one's for you, Bill Bradley!" a call which the youngster heard because Aspromonte and two of his teammates had also given him a transistor radio (and a pair of Colt .45 pajamas) during the visit. Had Shoeless Joe Jackson actually appeared out of the ether in left field that night it would have been regarded as only slightly less probable.

The sequel to the story is even more unlikely. The next year with his vision returning, Billy and his family sat behind the Houston dugout. He again asked for a home run and Aspromonte again promised only his best. This time, in a tie ballgame with two outs and the bases loaded in the bottom of the 10th Aspromonte hit a grand slam. You can look it up.

Several weeks later, Billy asked Bob for another home run. Laughing Aspromonte asked if a couple of hits would do. "No," was the reply. "You can do it, Bob. I *know* you can." (Children seem to know these things.) Of course, he did, and it was another grand slam. Billy, now seeing at 20-20 with contact lenses and playing Little League, went out and threw a no-hitter shortly thereafter, proclaiming for the local paper, "This one's for you, Bob Aspromonte!"[88]

Billy Bradley's hero stroked three walk-off home runs in a 13-year, 60 homer career, two of which were for his young admirer. His home run per request rate of 1.000 is significantly higher than his at-bats per home run rate. Maybe, Bob Aspromonte felt relaxed on those particular nights, his own life in a better perspective from his interactions with Billy. Maybe, Stu Miller and, for the record, Lindy McDaniel and Tracy Stallard respectively just didn't have it the nights they pitched. (Yes, that's the same Tracy Stallard who gave up Roger Maris' 61st home run.) Maybe Aspromonte was just due. There's probably a sabermetric actuarial table out there that would predict the probability of all this. *But still . . .*

The boy and the big leaguer, the former now a grown and successful adult and the latter now long retired would talk again—when Billy discovered that Bob Aspromonte had lost the vision in his right eye.

Life is an improbable sequence of events. The odds that we have the genes that we do, that we didn't maim or kill ourselves through any number of stupid things we did in adolescence, the haphazard way in which we find our spouses; these things constitute our lives, our being, and so they don't appear to be improbable. They're "just" the things that happened to us. It is Baseball, however, that showcases, then quantifies the improbable. It invites us to contemplate the improbable during a hot summer night for that second or two that the pitcher is in his stretch or on a cold winter's day while pouring over at-bats per home run ratios and discovering that tied with Mickey Mantle for 15th on the all-time list at 15.12 is Russell Branyon.

Our very existence is a miracle, really, at least a mathematical one, and the Universe, like baseball seems to run on math. The chance that one of those million sperm would find one of those 400 or so eggs (career total, of course) in a given environment are, let's see, carry the one . . . astronomical. And we haven't even calculated the odds of your father and mother ever meeting. Granted, there *is* a number that can be calculated that would predict our existence just as there is for Bob Aspromonte hitting three home runs on demand. The numbers are improbable, not infinite, but then none of us can grasp the meaning of *infinite*. The concept can't be expressed in numbers as one can always add one to whatever number you may conceive. Infinity can't be conceived of as space since space is really a word for the idea that there is nothing, but as soon as you say "There is" you contradict the idea of *nothing*. (Where's Yogi Berra when you need him?) *Infinity* is a one-word metaphor, really for something out there—and in here—that is greater than the self. It's "God within," a concept that exists in one form or another in every religion. It's that something that makes us say that a baseball team, for example, is greater than the sum of its parts.

Paul Tillich wrote in *The Dynamics of Faith* that "Man is able to understand in an immediate personal and central act the meaning of the ultimate, the unconditional, the absolute, the infinite. This alone makes faith a human potentiality. . . . Man is driven toward faith by his awareness of the infinite to which he belongs, but he does not own like a possession."[89]

Bob Aspromonte's home runs represent an "immediate personal and central act" because the improbable is a metaphor for the metaphor of infinity. That tiny number that represents the two-out, down by three in the bottom of the 9th grand slam brings us as close to the Infinite as anything in the modern world can. I suspect that it is no

76

accident that baseball became popular just as science was taking the mystery out of the world because baseball puts the magic back in our lives. We work the mute button and wear our lucky socks and don the same tee shirt during a winning streak in ritualistic behavior that is *directly* connected to the way in which we want to influence the world. Unlike so many other rituals performed in and out of churches today, those run-producing (or run-preventing) rituals have real meaning for those who perform them. I'm tired of understanding; I want to believe! Statistics I understand (mostly), but Oriole Magic I *believe!* Baseball people are mystics.

"The mystic is aware of the infinite distance between the infinite and the finite, and accepts a life of preliminary stages of union with the infinite, interrupted only rarely, and perhaps never, in this life by the final ecstasy," according to Tillich, who was clearly not a baseball person because if he were, he'd know that every game is interrupted by "the final ecstasy."[90] The center fielder who moves towards a long fly ball before the batter has even finished his swing, because he has fed a set of calculations into the fly ball computer in his head, magically transforming a double into an out represents *perfection!* Okay, so that may not be the "final ecstasy," but it's a moment *of* ecstasy. It's Roger Maris staring up at #61, still in flight. It's Brooks Robinson's game-winning single against the Twins; it's Marc Hyersion stepping onto the diamond at Bluefield for his first professional game; it's getting the assist on the final out of a perfect game. It's playing catch with your dad and teaching your daughter how to keep score. It's a white ball against a brilliant blue sky on the first truly warm day of spring.

It's returning to childhood once more.

I recall from my Sunday school days with Mr. Wade, a color illustration that appeared in most Bibles, of Jesus with a circle of children at his feet. This was inserted next to Matthew 19:14 which reads, "Jesus said, 'Let the little children come to me, and do not hinder them, for the kingdom of heaven belongs to such as these.'"[91] I never see a photo or newsreel footage of Babe Ruth with a gaggle of short-panted kids orbiting around him that I don't think of that Bible illustration.

Children are natural-born mystics. They *believe!* Again, it was Tillich who wrote, "Faith is the act in which reason reaches ecstatically beyond itself."[92] Children do this reflexively because their reason hasn't developed fully yet. It wasn't reasonable to think that Paul Blair could hit that home run off Claude Osteen, but because Reason would not get in the way, I was treated to "ecstasy beyond itself" if just for a moment. That moment, however, will live as long as I do, and, if somewhere out there or in here (collectively speaking) there is a repository for our yesterdays, it will live in Eternity.

This is exactly how Lizzy Kipps, one of my favorite Cub fans described it the day after Chicago won the World Series: "They'll live on in baseball lore, and in the hearts of Chicagoans, for as long as time endures." Interestingly, Lizzy didn't trust to "lucky socks or rituals" but to "the goodness of the team," adding,

To Cleveland, and other long-suffering fans in the sporting world, I say this: Don't give up. Don't lose heart. Hold your heads high and be patient. If it happened for us, it can happen for anyone. Never give up hope. It might take over a century, but it can happen, and the reward is greater than you can imagine.[93]

One might say that faith rewarded is a joy that passes all understanding. This is clearly demonstrated in the video that Lizzy took of herself and her family watching the bottom of the 10th inning of Game Seven. Posted to Facebook, Lizzy noted that the video's lighting wasn't good, but it seems perfect to me. A single light in the family living room, her dad Bruce on the couch to the left, her mom Becky in the middle, and Lizzy to her right. Out of the shot sits her brother, Andrew. The faces are barely distinguishable, but the ebb and flow of emotions in that bottom of the 10th are clearly visible. When the second out is recorded, Becky is almost overcome. "Oh, lord. Oh, my goodness," she says, her head in her hands. When Indian right-fielder Brandon Guyer steps to the plate, she instinctively reaches out both hands, one for Bruce, one for Lizzy, but the Davis single that scores Guyer who had walked, breaks their grasp. At this point, even the family cat can't take it and begins to scurry over floor and furniture. The cat doesn't understand videography and Lizzy has to pull him from in front of the camera. When Michael Martinez steps in representing the winning run for Cleveland, Becky, who has been on the edge of her chair, sits back ready to be swallowed up in its folds if the worst might happen. Martinez hits a slow chopper to third; off the bat it looks as if it might be a hit as announcer Joe Buck says, "This is going to be a tough play!" but third baseman Kris Bryant pounces on the ball and guns it to first base for the out. For a brief moment, the living room becomes a tableau, a look of disbelief, even confusion on Becky's face. Has she truly witnessed a miracle? Then a sudden jump and she and Lizzy are on their feet cheering.

"They did it!" Becky intones over and over again, through hugs and tears. "A team that we root for . . . did good!" she adds. She kisses Bruce's hand as Lizzy reaches for another tissue. Everyone sits back, drained. Perhaps *cleansed* is a better word. The home video closes with Joe Buck stating, "And the Cubs have won the World Series."[94]

***

"The emotional truths of childhood have a power to transcend objective fact. They stay with us through all the years, withstanding the ambivalence that so often accompanies the experiences of adults," so said, sportscaster Bob Costas in his eulogy for boyhood hero, Mickey Mantle.[95]

Reason gives us statistics; faith gives us ecstasy. Ecstasy is not the same thing as winning as Lizzy Kipps or any other Chicago Cubs fan will still tell you. The 1989 Orioles went from last to second, but not first. Ask any Oriole fan, however, and he or she will tell you that the "Why Not?" season was one of the most fun-filled glorious seasons in Baltimore baseball history. So many moments occurred in which reason reached beyond itself. Writing about the Orioles in July of that year, sportswriter Thomas Boswell sounded a great deal like theologian Paul Tillich:

Cynicism is just a mask we wear to protect the aging child inside. Given a chance, we would all rather tear away the disguise, at least for a while, and be childishly, ridiculously joyous. At the moment, the Orioles have become an excuse to reclaim some of what is left of our innocence—the part of our nature that is enthusiastic, pliable, even gullible. As long as the worst team in baseball (last year) is in or near first place, the laws of diminished wonder have been revoked.[96]

My difference with Boswell here is the use of the term "aging child inside." It is because the child inside never ages that we attempt to protect him with cynicism. "All baseball stems from childhood dreams."[97] So must all of life, but under the hot sun of modern life the dreams dry up and we are left with shallow little reminders of "all that was once good."

Instead of depth, we have a giant hole which we have attempted to fill with money, prestige, celebrity, possessions, drugs, statistics, self-righteousness, knowledge. We ignore that hole by covering it with a carpet of cynicism, yet step on the rug and fall into the same old hole. We wander, but rarely wonder. We want to touch the Unknown, but have convinced ourselves that we know everything or will soon enough. We want to believe, we *were built* to believe, but faith invites doubt, and doubt is not only troubling, but seemingly antiquated. Doubt is necessary to faith, of course, otherwise it's just blind obedience to somebody else's myth. After all, you may lose. The ecstasy of 1966 in Baltimore became the agony of 1969. Ecstasy is not winning.

It took me a good 40 years to get over the Orioles losing to the Miracle Mets in 1969. The Birds had won 109 games, were heavy favorites, and the Mets were baseball's proverbial laughing stock. After the Birds won the first game of the World Series, it seemed that we were on our way, but then miracles started happening. For them. Agee made impossible catches, J. C. Martin's bunt, Swoboda made the catch of his life, shutout relief by some scatter-armed flamethrower named Nolan Ryan. . . . When Dave Johnson flew out to left to end the last game and extinguish the faint hope of the greatest World Series comeback in history, I burst through the front door with my ball and glove and started throwing pop ups to myself. I didn't know what else to do. Your team doesn't always win, not even when they are the odds-on favorites. I kept throwing pop ups in an attempt to extinguish the anguish by exhausting myself. It didn't work.

Forty-three years later, however, I had the chance to talk to Oriole first baseman Boog Powell as part of a podcast and to my surprise, he told me that losing to the Mets didn't bother him (beyond the ordinary kind of bother that losing produces, of course). He said that the Mets played better, that the Orioles had been in a funk and barely beat the Twins in the playoffs, and that New York was a very good team. I looked it up. The Birds ended the regular season losing five of their final six, then beat Minnesota by only one run in each of the first two games, both of which went extra innings. The Mets had won 100 games. There's no doubt that today's modern statistical analysis would not have made the Orioles such heavy favorites in that series because of the Mets pitching. I still can't watch any highlights from that World Series, but at least I feel better now.

It's ironic that a mature statistical perspective was required to strengthen my faith, but what becomes clear is that faith is trust in a Grand Unknowable Process and not in an outcome. Sometimes, Mighty Casey strikes out, maybe even 2,597 times. We know he's going to fail 70% of the time, but the only time that counts is *this* time, and once we learn to see what it is we're looking at, then we see Magic *all* the time whether it's that center fielder getting a great jump on the ball or my daughter noting "FO:8" on her scorecard after the catch. The final score really doesn't have anything to do with it.

Yes, baseball has all the earmarks of a religion: gods, temples, relics. Baseball's enduring appeal, the reason it engenders such passion in its followers, however, is because it goes beyond religion. Campbell stated that, "The metaphor is the mask of God through which eternity is to be experienced."[98] Baseball is a metaphor. It is a *living* myth that puts us in touch with Eternity, with the Infinite. Its Miracle is not some long-ago act that contradicts the laws of physics. Its Miracle is the scrubbing away of cynicism to reveal the fresh-faced child within who is ready to believe, eager to believe, who *does* believe. Baseball people have experienced this Miracle; it is a by-product of their faith. It's only as children that we would dare ask Bob Aspromonte to hit a home run for us because it's only as children that we can perceive the Magic in the world.

The Self is a collection of selves and at 60 years of age, I have a dozen or so selves of various ages sitting around my Board of Directors table. Baseball has taught me to give the nine-year old director an equal voice. He should probably be named chairman.

***

I believe in the church of baseball. I've tried all the major religions and most of the minor ones. I've worshipped Buddha, Allah, Brahma, Vishnu, Shiva, trees, mushrooms, and Isadora Duncan. . . . I've tried them all, I really have. And, the only church that feeds the soul, day in, day out, is the church of baseball.[99]

So said the character of Annie Savoy in the film *Bull Durham*. If baseball has an apostles' creed this is it, even over and above Terrance Mann's speech in *Field of Dreams*.

Tillich, in writing about symbols of faith noted that "A great play gives us not only a new vision of the human scene, but it opens up hidden depths of our own being."[100] Of course I thought he had suddenly worked in a baseball reference, but eventually realized that he was talking about the theater and not Brooks Robinson in the 1970 World Series. Surely, art, ballet, opera, and theater inspire passion. There is magic in a performance or in a painting. Of course, to me, going to see the Mona Lisa is like going to a game of which you already know the final score. I already know what that painting looks like. In every game, however, there's the possibility that I'll see something that I've never seen before. Like a double-play sacrifice fly.

I also know that such an opinion might very well be my ignorance on the subject, and I can imagine that the trained eye might view a masterpiece every day and see something or feel something new each time. I am not trying convert anyone to the church of baseball, I'm just trying to explain it. Indeed, this is really just a "ballpark" explanation as I noted in the introduction. If you're over there on the third base side or in the upper deck or out in the bleachers, your point of reference will be different. Maybe you would refer to *The Natural* rather than *Shoeless Joe* to explain the church of baseball. Maybe you think Billy Cox was, or Adrian Beltre is a better third baseman than Brooks Robinson. That's okay. (You'd be wrong about Cox and Beltre, but that's okay.)

This is certainly no theology, which is the spiritual equivalent of geometry and about as exciting. In theology, you start with a premise such as "God exists" and extrapolate, establish corollaries and axioms (or is it axioms and corollaries?) until you have accomplished the impossible which is to make even God boring.

This is definitely no psychological examination of baseball although I've obviously made reference to psychology. We all know that 90% of this game is half-mental, as Yogi Berra once said and that sums it up pretty well.

This is a memoir. This is a personal recognition that baseball points to something I'll call God or Infinity or Eternity or Magic for short, something that is beyond my ability to comprehend, yet exists within me. And to paraphrase a line from another, much older book, "And *that* is good."

＊＊＊

And then there is Michael Lorenzen. The Cincinnati relief pitcher came on in the seventh inning of an August 19, 2016 game to extinguish a Dodger rally. He retired the two batters he faced; however, this was anything but a mundane relief appearance for a team going nowhere. Lorenzen's father Clif had died unexpectedly only two days before. When Lorenzen came in to warm up, "Who Are You?" by The Who—Clif's favorite band—played over the loud speaker. Upon retiring the side, Michael was so overcome with emotion that he had to duck into the clubhouse tunnel to compose himself. He needed to, for he was due up fifth in the inning and with the Reds up 6-1, there would be no need for a pinch-hitter. Sure enough, the Reds put two on and two out, and so Lorenzen, he of the three plate appearances all season, strode to the plate.

He drilled the first-pitch—a 97 miles per hour fastball from Pedro Baez—into the seats for a three-run homer. As he crossed the plate, he pointed to the sky, then pointed to his fiancé. He walked down the long congratulatory line of happy teammates until he reached the end where he found Ramon Cabrera, back-up catcher and Lorenzen's friend. Cabrera had purposely stationed himself at the end of the line. Lorenzen's hug was so strong, he almost knocked over Cabrera and the back-up catcher helped carry the pitcher's emotions.

Lorenzen returned to the mound after all this and turned in a scoreless eighth inning.

After the game, Cincinnati manager Bryan Price stated, "If you're around baseball and you've been here long enough, you'll see all sorts of things that you think you'll never see again or you never thought you would see. This falls under that heading. I never thought I would see something like that, as majestic and poetic and emotional as that moment."[101]

Fathers, sons, holy ghosts. See you at the ballpark.

***

"People ask me what I do in winter when there's no baseball. I'll tell you what I do. I stare out the window and wait for spring."—Rogers Hornsby, Hall of Fame second baseman.

ABOUT THE AUTHOR

Austin Gisriel has written several baseball books over the years including *Boots Poffenberger: Hurler, Hero, Hell-Raiser* (2014), and *Safe at Home: A Season in the Valley* (2009). *Their Glorious Summer* (2011) details the year that John Kruk, Dan Pasqua, and Tom Browning played in Virginia's Valley Baseball League, and it is available as a free download through any e-book store.

Please visit Austin's Amazon Author Page to leave a review of this work.

Follow his blog at www.austingisriel.com, on Facebook at "austinsauthropage," and on Twitter @AustinGisriel Austin enjoys and encourages interaction with his readers! Austin's biography may be found as a page on his blog.

Fathers, Sons, & Holy Ghosts: Baseball as a Spiritual Experience is also available as an e-book.

[1] Howard Sensel, *Baseball and the Cold War*, (New York: Harcourt, Brace, Jovanovich, 1977), 271. This is a fascinating book in which the author details growing up in 1950s Rochester, rooting for the Red Wings, becoming a left-wing activist, and while searching for true meaning in his life, rediscovers baseball.

[2] David Laurila, "Playing Catch and the 'Rhythm of the Universe,'" http://www.fangraphs.com/blogs/playing-catch-why-is-it-so-much-fun/, (August 31, 2011).

[3] Andrew Bailey has pitched for Oakland, Boston, the New York Yankees, Philadelphia and the Los Angeles Angels compiling a 3-1 record with 6 saves for the latter two teams in 2016. He was an All-Star in both 2009 & 2010.

[4] http://www.fangraphs.com/blogs/playing-catch-why-is-it-so-much-fun/

[5] Walter Otto, "Interpretation," in *Ways of Being Religious*, Frederick J. Streng, et. al. editors: (Englewood Cliffs, NJ, Prentice-Hall, Inc., 1973), 142.

[6] Joseph Campbell, *The Power of Myth with Bill Moyers*, Betty Sue Flowers, ed.: (New York: Doubleday, 1988), 5.

[7] Diane Ackerman, *Deep Play*, (New York: Random House, 1999), 12.

[8] Mac Faulkner, "Man drives 600 miles to listen to Cubs win with his father at his grave, keeping his promise," November 3, 2016, http://thechive.com/2016/11/03/man-drives-600-miles-to-listen-to-cubs-win-with-his-father-at-his-grave-keeping-his-promise-8-photos/

[9] Ackerman, 12.

[10] Ackerman, 105.

[11] Paul Tillich, "The Lost Dimension in Religion," in *Ways of Being Religious*, Frederick J. Streng, et. al. editors: (Englewood Cliffs, NJ, Prentice-Hall, Inc., 1973), 358.

[12] W. P. Kinsella, *Shoeless Joe*: (New York: Ballantine Books, 1982), 212. It is J. D. Salinger who delivers this soliloquy in the novel.

[13] *Field of Dreams: Twenty-five years later*, MLB Network Special, 2014.

[14] Alan Koontz, "Action isn't what baseball is really about," letter to the editor,

Morning Herald, October 2, 1992.

[15] *Field of Dreams: Twenty-five years later*

[16] *Ibid.*

[17] *Ibid.*

[18] Campbell, 223.

[19] Ackerman, 118.

[20] Sensel, 203-204.

[21] Anthony F. C. Wallace, "Rituals: Sacred and Profane—An Anthropological Approach," in *Ways of Being Religious,* Frederick J. Streng, et. al. editors: (Englewood Cliffs, NJ, Prentice-Hall, Inc., 1973), 157.

[22] If you don't know what these numbers mean, but you are still with me, then bless you, you are truly trying to understand what baseball is all about. Therefore, I am happy to explain that 511 is the record for most wins (by Cy Young), 56 is the longest hitting streak (by Joe DiMaggio in 1941), .406 is the last average over .400 (by Ted Williams, also in 1941), and 61 was the record for most home runs in a season by Roger Maris, set in 1961. Barry Bonds hit 73 in 2003, but he stands accused of using steroids and thus, his home run record is viewed by many as tainted.

[23] The Orioles would lose 8-7 in 11 innings with Doug Corbett absorbing the loss.

[24] Our first grandchild, Riley Harper Dice was born January 1, 2017.

[25] Rob Daniels, "Odd play works out for Hoppers," Greensboro *News and Record,* C1, C5, July 8, 2006.

[26] Emile Durkheim, "Religion as a Product of Social Need," in *Religion for a New Generation,* Jacob Needleman, et. al. editors: (New York: Macmillan Publishing Co., Inc., 1977), 69.

[27] *Ibid.*

[28] Paul Tillich, *Dynamics of Faith*: (New York: Harper Colophon Books, 1957), 29.

[29] Thomas Boswell, "The Bums of Summer," *Washington Post Magazine,*

March 26, 1989, 12-17 & 36.

[30] Thomas Boswell, "There's Joy in Birdland," *Washington Post Magazine*, July 9, 1989, 20-23.

[31] Karol V. Menzie, "Hey, Daddy, I Made The Bigs," *The Sun Magazine*, April 5, 1992.

[32] Or maybe it was those two games together when Brooks, Baltimore's Baseball Knight Errant, homered and then hit what we now term a "walk-off" single. Small sample size, as the sabermetricians say, but passion arises from the moment; it is not built one number at a time.

[33] David Noonan, "The Chicago Cubs, the Goat Curse, and the Psychological Roots of Superstition," https://www.scientificamerican.com/article/the-chicago-cubs-the-goat-curse-and-the-psychological-roots-of-superstition/, October 12, 2016

[34] I'm not sure what's wrong with the 1% that doesn't believe in such things. Something, though.

[35] Daniel Mano, "Giants fans blame even-year magic ending on Taylor Swift," http://www.mercurynews.com/2016/10/14/giants-fans-blame-even-year-magic-ending-on-taylor-swift/ October 14, 2016.

[36] Nic Flosi, "Cubs World Series celebration ranks as the 7th largest gathering in human history," http://www.fox32chicago.com/news/local/215601786-story, November 4, 2016.

[37] Stephen K. Sanderson, *Human Nature and the Evolution of Society*, (Boulder, CO: Westview Press, 2014), 359.

[38] WAR stands for "wins above replacement"; WHIP for "walks and hits per innings pitched; and ERA for "earned run average." If you're totally unfamiliar with these statistics, just substitute the word *numbers* in the textual sentence and you'll get the idea just fine.

[39] Thich Nhat Hanh is a Buddhist monk and leader of the modern mindfulness movement. See Plum Village.org http://plumvillage.org/about/thich-nhat-hanh/

[40] http://www.gcfa.org/trademarks

[41] John Thorn, "Ya Gotta Believe" in *Our Game*, http://ourgame.mlblogs.com/2011/06/16/ya-gotta-believe/, June 16, 2011.

[42] Rick Ankiel was a talented young pitcher who in 2000, started Game One of the NL Division Series against the Atlanta Braves. He lasted 2.2 innings, walking seven and throwing five wild pitches. He came undone right there on national television and did not recover, at least as a pitcher. In 2007 he returned to the Cardinals as an outfielder and played for several teams until retiring in 2013.

[43] Stephen D. Keener, "Too Much Baseball Is Not a Good Thing," http://www.littleleague.org/media/llnewsarchive/

[44] Sam Roberts, "Just How Long Does the Average Baseball Career Last?" *New York* Times, http://www.nytimes.com/2007/07/15/sports/baseball/15careers.html, July 15, 2007,

[45] Of course, a few of those 215 played exclusively before 1901. The number of players and the number of players in the Hall of Fame increases each year and not always in the same proportion, so we're close enough.

[46] Ted Williams, as told to John Underwood, *My Turn At Bat: The Story of My Life.* (New York: Pocket Books, 1969), 100.

[47] Tillich, *Dynamics of Faith,* p 12.

[48] Kinsella, 13.

[49] At least the 1982 Ballantine paperback edition is this long.

[50] Kinsella, 194.

[51] Kinsella, 198.

[52] O. Henry, "The Gift of the Magi."

[53] Bocock would play briefly for the San Francisco Giants and Philadelphia Phillies before retiring from professional baseball at the end of the 2014 season. Murphy has played for the New York Mets since 2008, making the National League All-Star team in 2014 and 2016. He was named NLCS MVP in 2015.

[54] Tillich, *Dynamics of Faith,* 102.

[55] I so enjoyed Rebel games, that I wrote *Safe at Home: A Season in the Valley* about the 2009 team and eventually became the webcaster for a stint. I also served a term on the Board of Directors.

[56] Exhorting Luis to go meant that we wanted to see him steal a base.

[57] David B. Stinson "Baltimore's American League Park: Original Home of the Future New York Yankees" http://deadballbaseball.com/

[58] Wikipedia. See also, Jim O'Brien, "At the Wall With Saul," in *Forbes Field: Essays and Memories of the Pirates Historic Ballpark, 1909-1971,* edited by David Cicotello and Angelo J. Louisa: (Jefferson, NC: McFarland, 2007), 150-153. It was O'Brien, a local author, who first reported Finkelstein's ritual.

[59] Mitch Album, *Heart of Detroit,* "Tom Derry" https://www.youtube.com/watch?v=iNrLNU5CuCI. Originally aired June 19, 2014 on Local 4 News.

[60] Dan Epstein, "Keepers of the Corner: The Navin Field Grounds Crew," *Rolling Stone,* http://www.rollingstone.com/culture/features/keepers-of-the-corner-the-navin-field-grounds-crew-20140917, September 17, 2014.

[61] Tom Derry in a blog post dated July 12, 2016 is still holding out some hope that the infield grass and dirt will be retained. http://navinfieldgroundscrew.blogspot.com/2016/07/the-end-of-era-comes-to-site-of.html

[62] Official Blog of the Navin Field Grounds Crew may be accessed at http://navinfieldgroundscrew.blogspot.com/

[63] Ira Zepp, *The Sacred Spaces of Westminster*: (Self-published, 1981), 10.

[64] Zepp, 23.

[65] Campbell, 215.

[66] http://en.wikipedia.org/wiki/Mandala

[67] Campbell, 216.

[68] Belinsky was a 25-year old rookie left-hander for the Los Angeles Angels when on May 5, 1962, he fired a no-hitter against the Baltimore Orioles. This was the fourth of five straight victories that began his major league career which reached its peak before June was over. A playboy who was linked to several Hollywood starlets and would in fact marry—and divorce—Playboy playmate Jo Collins, Belinsky ended 1962 with a 10-11 mark. He finished his major league career in early 1970 with a 28-51 mark, He succumbed to alcoholism, recovered, became a born-again Christian while living in Las Vegas, battled

bladder cancer, and died of a heart attack at age 64.

[69] Rev. Charles Mangan, "Church Teaching on Relics," *Catholic Education Resource Center*, 2003, http://www.catholiceducation.org/en/culture/catholic-contributions/church-teaching-on-relics.html.

[70] Erik Erikson. *Young Man Luther: A Study in Psychoanalysis and History:* (New York: W. W. Norton and Company, Inc., 1962), 187.

[71] Mark Twain, *The Innocents Abroad:* (New York: A Signet Classic, New American Library, 1966), 119-120.

[72] Never heard of Ted Lepcio? Well, from 1952-1961 he was a Red Sox, too, (and a White Sox, Twin, and Phillie) and hit .245 lifetime over 10 seasons which is a very respectable career. He, played the majority of his games at second base. No doubt there was some nine-year old who met Mr. Lepcio, got his autograph, treasured it, and now at aged 69 treasures the memory of Ted Lepcio (who is still living and 87) as much as others treasure the memory of Ted Williams.

[73] Nick Adenhart was just beginning to establish a promising big league career when he was killed in an auto accident following his fourth major league start.

[74] Sara Shahriari, "The Power of the World Works in Circles," *Indian Country*, http://indiancountrytodaymedianetwork.com/2012/03/11/power-world-works-circles-9973, March 11, 2012.

[75] John Eisenberg. "O's, fans share tears, memories," *The Sun*, October 7, 1991, A1.

[76] Sensel, 15-16.

[77] Dick Schaap, "The Man Who Would Not Quit," *Parade Magazine*, August 7, 1983, 12-13.

[78] Email from Bob Williams, sent January 10, 2015.

[79] Marc Gunther, "A 'Baby Bird' Tries His Wings," *The Sun Magazine*, August 21, 1983, 7-11 & 26-28.

[80] Campbell, 161

[81] Patrick A. McGuire, "The Man Behind The Ironman Image," *Sun Magazine*, March 25, 1990, 8-13.

[82] *Ibid* 132

[83] Although, the concept of designating someone to hit for the pitcher goes back to the 19th century.

[84] See for example, *Baseball's Biggest Miracle: The 1914 Boston Braves*, (SABR, fall 2012) by Frank Ceresi and John B. Holway.

[85] Keith Robbins, "Historical Hitter October 6, 1926: Babe Ruth," *Be a Better Hitter*, http://www.beabetterhitter.com/historical-hitter-october-6-1926-babe-ruth/

[86] Nicholas Hirshon, "Babe Ruth's home run vow to New Jersey boy confirmed," *Daily News*, http://www.nydailynews.com/sports/baseball/yankees/babe-ruth-home-run-vow-sick-jersey-boy-confirmed-article-1.293847, June 19, 2008.

[87] John G. Hubbell, "The Little Leaguer and the Big Leaguer," *Reader's Digest*, April 1992, 81-85.

[88] *Ibid.*

[89] Tillich, *Dynamics of Faith,* 9.

[90] *ibid*

[91] From *The New International Version* which, certainly in the case of this verse, provides a meaningful and vibrant translation.

[92] Tillich, *Dynamics of Faith,* p 16.

[93] Instant message from Lizzy Kipps, November 3, 2016. Lizzy believed in the team, but that's not to say she was calm "at any point throughout the game." Faith, of course, does not require tranquility, just steadfastness.

[94] The Kipps family is a true baseball family. Becky coordinates the post-game meals for the New Market Rebels while Andrew and older sister Anna serve on the Rebels' Board of Directors. Anna and her husband Jimmy also host players for the summer while Andrew is New Market's official scorer. Lizzy, a quiet, but ardent fan helps her dad, Bruce, maintain the family's sanity during the Rebels summer seasons.

[95] Taken from the Associated Press report of Bob Costas' eulogy of Mickey Mantle, delivered August 15, 1995. It appeared in many newspapers the next day, including Hagerstown's *Morning Herald* on p D4 of the Sports section.

[96] Thomas Boswell, "There's Joy in Birdland," *Washington Post Magazine,* July

9, 1989, p 20-23.

[97] Howard Sensel, *Baseball and the Cold War*, p 146.

[98] Joseph Campbell with Bill Moyers, *The Power of Myth*, p 60.

[99] *Bull Durham*, screenplay by Ron Shelton, 1988.

[100] Tillich, *Dynamics of Faith*, p 42.

[101] Zach Buchanan, "Lorenzen homers in first game since father's death," cincinnati.com, http://www.cincinnati.com/story/sports/mlb/reds/2016/08/19/lorenzen-homers-first-game-since-fathers-death/89032192/ August 20, 2016.

Made in the USA
Lexington, KY
14 October 2018